The DIY CFO

The DIY CFO

Financial Strategies for Small Businesses Without Accountants – Runs through financial planning in plain English.

Kenji Takahashi

Mindful Pages

Published in 2026

ISBN: 9789374120620 (PB)
ISBN: 9789374121245 (eBook)

Published by

Mindful Pages
Imprint of Alpha Editions LLC
312 W. 2nd St #1834
Casper, WY 82601, USA

This book was developed using advanced writing tools to support the drafting and ideation process. All content has been thoughtfully curated, refined, and reviewed to ensure quality and relevance.

Content

Introduction

The DIY CFO: Financial Strategies for Small Businesses Without Accountants

On a grey January morning in Birmingham, a café owner sits at her small wooden counter, staring at the numbers on her laptop. The café is full, every table taken, the till brimming with sales receipts. Yet her stomach knots. The bank balance tells a different story: overdraft charges, supplier bills piling up, and a payroll run due in three days. How can a business so busy feel so broke? She has no accountant on hand, no finance team in the back office—only herself, her laptop, and her instinct. She is already making decisions that could save or sink her company. She just doesn't yet recognise them as the work of a Chief Financial Officer.

Her story is not unique. Across Britain and far beyond, founders, freelancers, and family businesses live this paradox. They are lauded for their ingenuity, yet often undone not by competition or customer demand, but by the invisible mechanics of finance. Profit on paper does not mean cash in the bank. A surge in sales can, perversely, hasten collapse. The rhythm of money through a business—when it enters, when it leaves, and how it flows in between—remains for many a mystery. And when the mystery turns urgent, too many small businesses discover too late that their rear-view statements, neatly filed for tax compliance, offer no map for the road ahead.

This book begins with a simple assertion: you are already the CFO of your business, whether you acknowledge it or not. Every choice you make—setting prices, negotiating terms, deciding when to hire, whether to extend credit—is a financial decision. The question is not whether you wear the CFO's hat, but whether you wear it consciously.

The Problem Hidden in Plain Sight

Small businesses form the backbone of every economy. They employ vast swathes of the population, fuel innovation, and sustain communities. Yet they are also fragile. In the United Kingdom, more than half of new businesses fail within five years. In the United States, the figure is scarcely better. The leading cause, study after study confirms, is not poor products or lack of demand but cash mismanagement. It is not that entrepreneurs cannot do maths. It is that they are given the wrong tools, or no tools at all, for the real work of financial command.

Too often, finance is reduced to bookkeeping—a compliance exercise in recording what has already happened, designed primarily for the tax authority or the bank manager. That record has its place, but it does little to help a founder decide whether to raise prices, which client to prioritise, or whether they can afford to take on a new hire this quarter. Looking backwards may keep you compliant; it does not keep you alive.

The real levers of financial control—working capital, unit economics, operating cadence—rarely appear in statutory reports. And so many founders run blind. They mistake activity for control, growth for health, profit for cash. Until, like the café owner, they are caught between a crowded room and an empty account.

A Timeless Challenge

This tension between profit and cash, between growth and survival, is not new. Venetian merchants of the fifteenth century wrestled with it when deciding how to finance voyages that might last years. Textile mills in the Industrial Revolution expanded too quickly, only to find their creditors calling in debts before finished goods could be sold. Even the great railroads of the nineteenth century, symbols of progress and abundance, were perpetually on the brink of collapse—not because passengers failed to ride, but because the capital cycle demanded cash faster than fares could be collected.

History reminds us that finance has always been less about arithmetic and more about timing, trust, and foresight. The balance between inflows and outflows, between promises made and promises met, has undone empires and bankrupted kings. What has changed is not the essence of the problem, but the scale and the tools available to solve it. Today's entrepreneur has spreadsheets instead of ledgers, online dashboards instead of clerks—but the same fundamental truths endure. Cash is still the drumbeat. Contribution still trumps vanity. And the courage to act before the crisis still separates survival from ruin.

What This Book Offers

This book does not ask you to become an accountant. It does not drown you in jargon or expect you to spend your evenings lost in reconciliation. What it does is teach you to see finance as a set of levers you can pull, rather than a ledger you must endure. It gives you a small number of forward-looking tools, each designed to increase your decision bandwidth. With fewer, clearer metrics, you will find you can focus, act, and lead.

Across these chapters, you will learn how to:

Establish a weekly operating cadence that transforms finance from panic to practice.

Build a 13-week cash model that predicts, rather than reacts to, your business's survival.

Identify the unit economics that truly decide whether your company lives or dies.

Set prices and terms that protect margin and stabilise cash.

Create simple board packs that cut through vanity and drive action.

Each idea is rooted in practice, illustrated with cases drawn from cafés, agencies, manufacturers, and software companies. Each is designed to be implemented with nothing more than a spreadsheet, a pen, and an hour a week.

A Motif: The Drumbeat

Consider cash as a drumbeat. It is not the melody of your business—that is your product, your people, your vision—but it is the rhythm that keeps everything moving. Lose the beat, and the music falters, however brilliant the melody. Keep it steady, and you can layer complexity, harmony, and improvisation on top.

This drumbeat is the metaphor we will return to throughout the book. It reminds us that finance is not abstract. It is not numbers on a page. It is movement, rhythm, flow. Each decision either strengthens or disrupts that beat. Your task as the DIY CFO is not to play every instrument, but to keep the rhythm steady enough for the rest of the band to play.

Why Urgent, Why Now

Why does this matter more than ever today? Because the environment in which small businesses operate has grown harsher and faster. Supply chains stretch across continents and snap without warning. Customers pay later, while expenses—rent, wages, software subscriptions—remain stubbornly immediate. Digital platforms enable rapid growth, but that growth magnifies mistakes as quickly as it magnifies success. In this world, a founder who cannot see thirteen weeks ahead is perpetually hostage to the bank balance.

Moreover, access to external finance is shifting. Banks are cautious, investors demanding, and new funding instruments—from revenue-based finance to crowdfunding—require sharper understanding of risk and return. To engage with these sources on your own terms, not theirs, you must first command your own numbers.

Looking Ahead

The chapters that follow will not only equip you with technical tools but will reshape the way you see your business. You will come to understand that every invoice, every payment term, every pricing choice is not a detail but a lever of survival. You will discover that financial clarity does not restrict your creativity but enables it, freeing you to take risks from a position of strength.

As you turn the page, ask yourself:

What if financial control is not about more information, but about the right information?
What if the difference between thriving and folding lies not in strategy or vision, but in the rhythm of cash?
And what if, far from being a burden, taking command of your business's finances could become the most liberating act of all?

This book is your guide to answering those questions. By its end, you will not only survive as your own CFO—you will thrive. The drumbeat awaits.

Chapter 1
The CFO You Already Are

On a Tuesday evening in Leeds, a young designer locks up her studio, lights still glowing over the desks. The day has been relentless: client calls, deadlines, a new proposal sent out. Yet as she sits down with her notebook at home, she cannot shake the unease. There is money coming in, invoices sent and logged, but the bank account looks thin. She is confident in her craft, admired by her clients, even envied by her peers—but she cannot answer the simplest of questions: do I have enough to pay my staff next month? She has never called herself a Chief Financial Officer. She barely uses the phrase. And yet, every choice she makes about prices, about hiring, about how quickly to chase late payments—that is exactly what a CFO does.

This quiet contradiction plays out daily in small businesses across the world. Founders and owners imagine the CFO as a distant figure in a grey suit, someone reserved for corporations with departments and directors. They picture financial control as something external: the domain of accountants, banks, and reports filed away at year's end. Meanwhile, in the texture of ordinary days, they themselves are deciding whether to extend credit, whether to invest in growth, whether to take on a risk they cannot yet afford. They are already the CFO. The question is whether they act knowingly, or blindly.

It is tempting to believe that compliance is control—that once the books are balanced, the tax returns filed, and the statements printed, one has command of the numbers. But this is an illusion. Compliance looks backwards; control looks forwards. The ledger records what has happened; the levers shape what happens next. Bookkeeping is essential, yes, but it is the scaffolding, not the structure. To mistake one for the other is to confuse the rear-view mirror with the steering wheel. You need both, but only one will keep you on the road ahead.

Finance, at its heart, is the art of turning complexity into choice. Yet most founders drown themselves in too many numbers, mistaking data for insight. They track revenue, costs, overheads, tax, gross profit, net profit, and countless ratios besides, until their decision bandwidth collapses under the weight. Paradoxically, the more they measure, the less they act. The work of the CFO is to reverse this: to strip away the noise, to select the few metrics that matter, and to see them not as static figures but as levers for motion. Decisions are not made in the clutter; they are made in the clarity.

Behavioural science offers a simple lesson: what we attend to, we act upon. If a team is told to watch revenue, they will chase it—often at the cost of margin, cash, or sanity. If instead they are asked to monitor contribution margin—the money left after true variable costs—they will make different decisions. They will price with confidence, decline unprofitable work, retain customers more carefully. The focus becomes a steering wheel rather than a scoreboard. The act of measuring changes the act of managing. That is why this chapter will ask you to define one movement metric for each function of your business. Not ten, not five—one. Because attention, when narrowed, creates motion.

The most treacherous illusion in finance is the distinction between profit and cash. Profit is seductive, because it looks like truth. It appears tidy on a statement, precise to the pound, calculated according to accepted rules. But profit is an opinion until the cash clears. Accruals can flatter, timing differences can mislead, growth itself can become a parasite that drains cash faster than it generates it. Many businesses have collapsed while reporting profits, starved of the liquidity to pay suppliers or staff. This is not a flaw of accounting; it is a flaw of perception. The antidote is perspective—a 13-week horizon that reveals not just whether the business is profitable, but whether it can survive the quarter. Profit can lie to you; cash will not.

And then, there is rhythm. Businesses that thrive financially are not those with the most elaborate spreadsheets, but those with a simple cadence: one hour, once a week, with the same four questions and the same scoreboard. A founder and their small team, no matter how small, can carve out this space. They review, they decide, they act. The meeting is not a ritual to impress, but a practice to move. In this rhythm lies the true shift: finance becomes not an annual panic or a quarterly puzzle, but a weekly discipline woven into the fabric of the company.

What follows in this chapter is not a manual for accountants but a map for decision-makers. You will learn to distinguish the mirror from the wheel, the ledger from the lever. You will see how to choose metrics that matter, how to distrust profit when it flatters, how to treat cash as the truth beneath the noise. And you will encounter the operating cadence that ties it all together—so that finance stops being a language you dread, and becomes the rhythm by which your business moves.

The role of the CFO is already yours. This chapter will show you how to wear it with intent. Turn the page, and you will find that the numbers you once feared are not walls but doors—doors into clarity, command, and control. The decision is already yours; the difference is whether you make it on purpose.

From compliance to command

At the turn of the twentieth century, Henry Ford walked the factory floor of his new automobile plant and saw what few others could. While bookkeepers tallied wages, parts, and sales long after the fact, Ford cared about something else: the rhythm of production, the flow of materials, the rate at which finished cars left the line. His focus was not on the ledger but on the levers—the mechanisms he could adjust today to alter tomorrow. That distinction, between recording and controlling, between compliance and command, remains as vital for the smallest business as it was for the industrial giant.

Most founders mistake bookkeeping for control. They see the pile of reconciled receipts, the completed VAT return, the tidy profit and loss statement, and feel reassured that their financial house is in order. Yet compliance is not command. Bookkeeping is retrospective, a mirror of what has happened. Control, by contrast, is prospective: it is the deliberate use of financial information to influence what will happen next. A ledger is a record; a lever is an instrument of power. Confusing the two is why so many owners feel busy yet powerless, informed yet unable to act.

Consider the paradox of information overload. In theory, more data should produce better decisions. In practice, it often paralyses. Behavioural scientists call this the "paradox of choice": when presented with too many options, humans tend to defer action, fall back on habit, or spread their attention thinly across the noise. Business leaders are no different. Faced with a dashboard of twenty metrics, they flit from one to another, mistaking motion for momentum. The concept of *decision bandwidth* reframes the problem. Just as a radio signal becomes clearer when tuned to one frequency, decision-making sharpens when the number of monitored metrics is reduced. Command is not about drowning in numbers; it is about selecting the few that matter, then acting on them relentlessly.

One vivid example comes from a mid-sized software company in Manchester. For years, management had obsessed over top-line revenue, celebrating every new customer. Yet despite impressive growth, margins eroded and cash dwindled. When they shifted focus to contribution margin per client—the money remaining after variable costs of servicing each account—they discovered that their most celebrated contracts were quietly destroying value. Within three months of refocusing their attention, they altered pricing structures, shed loss-making accounts, and restored financial health. The insight was not hidden in the accounts; it was hidden in plain sight, obscured by the wrong choice of metric.

Metrics, after all, are not neutral. They direct attention, shape culture, and determine action. A sales team chasing revenue will discount heavily, chase volume, and ignore cost. The same team, when measured on contribution margin, will negotiate more carefully, protect pricing power, and walk away from toxic deals. What we measure becomes movement. The selection of metrics is therefore not merely technical; it is profoundly behavioural. Leaders must recognise that every metric chosen sends a signal about what matters, and that signal ripples through decisions at every level of the business.

This is why forward-looking tools matter so profoundly. Rear-view statements—the profit and loss account, the balance sheet—are essential for compliance but dangerously deceptive when used for navigation. They tell you where you have been, not where you are going. A driver who stares only into the rear-view mirror may be compliant with the rules of record-keeping, but will not stay on the road. Command requires instruments oriented to the future: cash-flow forecasts, leading indicators, operating cadences. These are not about recording the past but about shaping the path ahead.

The distinction becomes urgent when growth enters the picture. Growth, by its nature, is cash-hungry. More customers mean more inventory, more staff, more upfront cost—all before the revenue is collected. To mistake a rising profit line for security is to fall into the classic trap of "profitable bankruptcy." Countless businesses have collapsed while technically profitable, because their bank accounts could not sustain the lag between sales and cash. Compliance will not warn you of this danger. Command will. By building forward-looking views—thirteen-week cash projections, working capital analyses—you see the cliff edge before you reach it.

Agency is the essence of command. Too many founders imagine that finance is something that happens to them: dictated by the bank, explained by the accountant, constrained by the ledger. Yet every decision they make—whether to hire, to discount, to delay payment, to renegotiate terms—is a financial choice. They already hold the levers, even if they do not yet see them as such. To recognise this is liberating. It shifts the mindset from passive recipient of financial fate to active shaper of financial outcomes. The café owner who insists on deposits before large catering orders, the freelancer who refuses to bill monthly in arrears, the small manufacturer who monitors contribution margin per machine hour—each is practising command, not compliance.

The danger is subtle but profound: a business can appear orderly on paper while drifting rudderless in practice. Ledgers will never prevent drift, because they are not designed to. Levers do. They allow you to alter the course in real time, to translate numbers into action. The act of command is not about complexity but about clarity. It is the discipline of asking: which three numbers, if I monitored them every week, would change how I act next week? The answer is rarely revenue or profit. It is cash, contribution, and cadence—the measures that connect today's decision to tomorrow's survival.

This distinction between compliance and command is not academic. It is the difference between businesses that endure and those that falter. It is the difference between the founder who sees finance as a burden and the one who uses it as a source of agency. To treat finance as a ledger is to consign yourself to passivity. To treat it as a set of levers is to embrace the responsibility—and the freedom—of control.

The question, then, is simple but uncomfortable: if you are already making CFO-level choices, why not make them on purpose? The levers are in your hands whether you acknowledge them or not. The only decision left is whether to pull them with intent, or allow them to move at random. The path to command begins the moment you stop mistaking the mirror for the wheel.

What we measure becomes movement

In the 1950s, General Motors boasted some of the highest revenues in the world. It measured sales above all else and celebrated volume as proof of dominance. Yet as profits thinned and customer loyalty waned, the obsession with revenue blinded executives to a harsher truth: what they had gained in turnover they had lost in margin. They had measured the wrong thing, and so they moved in the wrong direction. The same trap, writ smaller, ensnares thousands of modern businesses. When attention is fixed on numbers that cannot be controlled, action drifts. When focus shifts to metrics tied to behaviour, movement follows.

The paradox is simple: numbers do not just reflect behaviour—they shape it. Behavioural science has long shown that what we monitor and reward alters what we do. Psychologists call it the "Hawthorne effect": workers' productivity rose merely because they knew they were being observed. Economists frame it as Goodhart's Law: when a measure becomes a target, it ceases to be a good measure, because people bend their actions to meet it. In business, the lesson is direct: choose a metric badly, and you will distort behaviour in damaging ways. Choose it well, and you unlock a predictable current of motion.

Revenue is the most seductive bad metric of all. It feels tangible, impressive, and easy to track. Founders beam when sales rise and despair when they fall. Yet revenue is not value. A pound of revenue from one customer may cost more to deliver than it earns, while another customer, paying less, may contribute far more to the firm's survival. Chasing revenue at all costs leads to frantic discounting, over-servicing, and a culture where "winning the deal" matters more than sustaining the business.

Contribution margin, by contrast, is grounded in reality. It asks: after covering the direct costs of serving this customer, delivering this product, or fulfilling this contract, what remains to cover the overheads and generate profit? This measure cuts through vanity and forces clarity. A company that shifts focus from revenue to contribution margin will often discover uncomfortable truths—celebrated "big wins" that secretly destroy value, small clients that quietly fund the whole enterprise. But in that discomfort lies agency. Once you see contribution margin, you can act: adjust pricing, improve terms, redesign offers, or walk away from toxic accounts.

A design agency in Bristol offers a striking example. For years, its leadership obsessed over total billings. They had charts showing monthly revenue, tracked daily sales, and celebrated when the firm crossed symbolic thresholds. Yet despite hitting those numbers, cash reserves never grew, and staff turnover increased. When they recalibrated their focus to contribution margin per project, the picture changed. They discovered that long, fixed-fee projects for large clients yielded less per hour than short, high-intensity assignments for smaller firms. The team shifted its business model—fewer vanity accounts, more of the profitable shorter work. Within six months, not only had their margins recovered, but their staff were less burnt out and their cash position stabilised. By changing what they measured, they changed how they moved.

The principle extends beyond finance. In human systems, attention is the most powerful currency. A sales team told to measure "calls made" will dutifully make calls, often of poor quality, to hit the target. The same team told to measure "qualified proposals accepted" will behave differently: they will research prospects, focus on fit, and pursue genuine opportunities. An operations team told to measure "units produced" may cut corners to maximise output. Told instead to measure "units delivered without rework," they will focus on quality and sustainable throughput. Every measure is a magnet; it pulls behaviour towards itself.

This is why the discipline of selecting one *movement metric* per function is so potent. In sales, it might be contribution margin per deal. In marketing, it could be cost per qualified lead. In customer success, perhaps churn within 90 days of onboarding. The point is not to find the perfect number but to pick one that is both actionable and consequential. By narrowing attention to a single, well-chosen measure, teams align effort, reduce noise, and create predictable motion. Decision bandwidth, previously scattered, converges.

The philosophy here runs deeper than management technique. It touches on the way humans create meaning. We are storytelling creatures, and metrics are among the most powerful stories we tell ourselves. They signal what we value, they anchor our sense of progress, and they justify our actions. To measure revenue is to tell the story of growth, regardless of cost. To measure contribution margin is to tell the story of sustainability. To measure churn is to tell the story of loyalty. Each story generates behaviours that make the narrative come true. In this sense, metrics are not mere reflections; they are self-fulfilling prophecies.

Yet caution is warranted. Metrics can easily calcify into dogma. A company that idolises margin to the exclusion of all else may neglect long-term growth or innovation. A business that obsesses over churn may hesitate to experiment with bold but risky ideas. The art of command lies not in finding one eternal metric but in revisiting and revising them as the context changes. Metrics are levers, not idols. Their purpose is to direct movement, not to become monuments.

Still, the contrast between measuring revenue and measuring contribution margin illustrates the core truth: when attention shifts, behaviour shifts. By extension, the future shifts. What we measure becomes movement. A founder who recognises this wields extraordinary power. The danger is not ignorance but distraction—the temptation to monitor everything, to drown in dashboards, to confuse visibility with control. Clarity requires discipline. The discipline of less.

And so a question lingers. If every measure is a magnet for behaviour, if every number we track reshapes the path we walk, then what single measure should you choose for each function of your business? Not the one that flatters, but the one that changes how you act. Not the one that looks good in a pitch deck, but the one that keeps the rhythm of cash and value steady. In the end, the numbers will always move. The only choice is whether they move you forward—or lead you astray.

Cash vs profit (and why one lies to you)

In the summer of 2019, a London-based food delivery start-up announced record profits. Investors cheered, headlines praised the triumph, and staff were promised bonuses. Yet within months the company was gone. Suppliers went unpaid, riders complained of missing wages, and administrators arrived to liquidate what was left. On paper the business had been profitable; in reality it had no cash. The profit figure had been a mirage, a comforting abstraction that masked the simple truth: you cannot spend profit, only cash.

This paradox—profitable but bankrupt—has undone companies large and small for centuries. Profit is a construct, governed by accounting conventions, accruals, and assumptions. It is an opinion, not a fact, until money clears the bank. Cash, by contrast, is brutally honest. It arrives or it doesn't. It pays staff or it doesn't. It covers rent, tax, and suppliers—or it doesn't. In business, survival is measured not in profits declared but in cash available. Yet many founders continue to mistake one for the other, and by the time they grasp the difference, it is too late.

The first culprit is timing. Profit and cash rarely move in step. You may record revenue the moment you issue an invoice, but cash arrives only when the customer pays—weeks, sometimes months later. Expenses, meanwhile, can outpace income. You might order inventory, pay staff, or settle supplier bills long before the customer's money lands. The ledger shows profit; the bank balance shows strain. These timing differences accumulate, stretching cash like an elastic band until it snaps.

Accrual accounting deepens the trap. It smooths reality, allocating revenues and costs to the periods in which they are deemed to belong, rather than when cash actually moves. This provides a fairer picture for long-term reporting, but it lulls founders into complacency. A contractor may book the full value of a project as revenue in January, even though the client will pay in staggered instalments over the year. On paper, the month looks profitable; in practice, January's bills could outrun January's receipts. Accruals are useful for compliance but dangerous as a compass. They obscure the very thing that matters most: liquidity today.

The danger escalates with growth. Growth consumes cash before it produces it. A retailer opening a second store must pay for rent, fit-out, stock, and staff months before sales arrive. A software firm onboarding a flood of new customers must expand servers, support teams, and onboarding staff, often before the first subscription payment clears. On paper, the income statement glows:

revenue rising, profit margins widening. In reality, the cash curve plunges. Growth starves cash, and unless managed with precision, the company suffocates under its own expansion. This is the cruel irony: the faster you grow, the closer you edge to insolvency.

The early warning signs are subtle. Suppliers calling for payment extensions, staff salaries met a day late, overdrafts creeping higher each month. These are not accidents; they are symptoms of cash starvation. Yet too many leaders ignore them, seduced by profit figures that suggest health. The bank balance is dismissed as a temporary blip, the cash crunch rationalised as "seasonal." By the time the gravity of the situation is undeniable, options are few.

The antidote is not more complex accounting but a simpler discipline: the 13-week cash horizon. Thirteen weeks—one quarter—is long enough to see risks emerging, short enough to manage actively. Unlike annual budgets or five-year plans, which are exercises in speculation, the 13-week view deals in near-term reality. What cash is in the bank today? What payments are due this week? What inflows are genuinely expected, and when? Each line is tied to a date, an owner, and a level of certainty. The forecast is reconciled weekly against actuals, creating a rhythm of truth. Variances are not failures but lessons, sharpening judgement with each cycle.

A Midlands manufacturer illustrates the power of this horizon. For years, management relied on profit reports and quarterly statements. Every year they showed modest profits; every year they scrambled for emergency overdrafts. Only when they built a 13-week cash forecast did the pattern emerge: seasonal orders spiked inventory purchases in September, draining cash, while customers consistently paid 30 days later than expected. By seeing the rhythm clearly, they renegotiated supplier terms, adjusted production schedules, and stabilised cash. Profit had told them they were safe; cash had warned them they were not.

The truth is both humbling and liberating. Cash strips away illusion. It ignores accruals, shrugs at accounting finesse, and demands only clarity: money in, money out, balance left. It tells you what you can and cannot do. For founders, embracing cash as the central measure is not an act of pessimism but of agency. It grounds ambition in reality, ensuring that growth is funded, obligations met, and opportunities seized without fear of collapse.

Yet the tension remains. Profit will always seduce with its polish, cash will always confront with its bluntness. The discipline is to resist the siren call of flattering profit figures and listen instead to the drumbeat of liquidity. The ledger may whisper that you are thriving; the bank balance may shout that you are not. Which will you believe? More importantly, which will you act upon?

The answer lies in rhythm. The business that reviews cash weekly, projects thirteen weeks ahead, and treats every variance as information is the business that survives. But survival is not the end in itself. The deeper question is this: if profit can deceive and cash can constrain, how can you build a system where both work together—not as rivals, but as guides? The path forward demands more than vigilance; it demands design. And that design begins with the cadence of decisions yet to come.

A weekly operating cadence

Every Friday morning, in a small workshop in Sheffield, the owner and her two apprentices sit around a battered oak table. The ritual is always the same. They open the ledger of jobs completed, glance at the bank balance, and ask four questions: What came in? What went out? What is due next week? What needs to change? The meeting lasts less than an hour, but its rhythm is unwavering. It is not a performance for an accountant, nor a formality for the bank. It is the pulse of the business itself. The practice seems modest, almost trivial, yet it is precisely this cadence that has kept the workshop solvent and stable through recessions, supplier collapses, and even a global pandemic.

The paradox is that most small businesses spend more time producing reports than making decisions. Endless hours vanish into spreadsheets, slide decks, and updates designed to satisfy external parties. Numbers are collected, collated, and presented, but rarely interrogated. The result is ritual without consequence. A weekly cadence, properly designed, breaks this cycle. It shifts finance from a retrospective exercise into a living discipline, embedded in the operating fabric of the company. The rule is simple: one hour, once a week, the same questions, the same scoreboard. Predictability is its power.

The cadence forces clarity because it creates scarcity. One hour is not enough time for sprawling reports or tangential debates. It requires selectivity: only the numbers that matter, only the issues that demand action. Decision bandwidth is preserved, not wasted. A founder who knows that cash flow will be reviewed every Friday cannot delay unpleasant truths until quarter-end. A team that expects to discuss contribution margin weekly cannot hide behind vague revenue wins. The short, relentless rhythm builds discipline, just as athletes improve not through occasional effort but through repeated drills.

The structure of the meeting is deceptively simple. A scoreboard of the agreed metrics—cash balance, inflows, outflows, contribution per unit, leading indicators—is presented at the start. The numbers are not explained at length; they are compared to expectations. Four questions follow. What changed this week? What will happen next week? Where are we off track? What decisions must be taken? Each question has an owner, even in a two-person team. If cash collection is behind, someone owns the calls. If a pricing shift is needed, someone drafts the change. The meeting ends with commitments dated and recorded. Without commitments, the cadence decays into ceremony. With them, it becomes motion.

Consider the contrast with companies that neglect such a rhythm. A London-based digital agency once prided itself on creativity but avoided financial scrutiny. Monthly reviews dragged into three-hour marathons, crammed with charts but empty of decisions. Problems festered unnoticed: late-paying clients, projects delivered at a loss, cash reserves evaporating. When the reckoning came, it seemed sudden, but it was not. It was the cumulative effect of weeks without discipline. Had the agency adopted a weekly cadence, the warning signs would have surfaced early enough to act.

The philosophical insight is that time structures behaviour. Humans are creatures of rhythm; we align our actions to the intervals we set. An annual budget invites annual surprises. A quarterly review invites quarterly shocks. A weekly cadence invites weekly course correction, making crises smaller and more manageable. The choice of rhythm is, in effect, the choice of resilience. Businesses with short cadences absorb turbulence; those with long cadences accumulate it.

Even the smallest teams benefit. A sole trader who spends an hour each week confronting inflows and outflows, forecasting thirteen weeks ahead, will act with more confidence than a founder who glances sporadically at the bank app. In larger firms, the discipline scales. Cross-functional teams can align around shared metrics, preventing finance from becoming a siloed concern. Marketing, sales, operations—all tethered to the same scoreboard—see their actions reflected in the company's cash rhythm. The meeting becomes the junction where strategy meets reality.

The risk, of course, is that routine becomes rote. A cadence stripped of urgency degenerates into ritual reporting. To prevent this, the focus must remain on decisions, not documents. Every number on the scoreboard must carry an implied question: *What will we do differently because of this?* If no action follows, the metric is noise. The meeting ends not when time is exhausted but when every decision has an owner and a deadline.

History offers its own lesson in cadence. The Venetian merchants of the Renaissance, who financed voyages across uncertain seas, gathered weekly to review ledgers, debts, and cargo returns. Their rhythm allowed them to anticipate shortages, renegotiate credit, and redeploy capital. They knew that fortune favoured not the boldest but the most disciplined. Their weekly rituals built empires that endured for centuries. Modern founders, though armed with dashboards and cloud software, face the same truth: without rhythm, information drifts into inertia.

The weekly cadence is not an administrative detail; it is the architecture on which every financial tool in this book depends. Without it, the 13-week forecast is a static file, the unit economics a forgotten exercise, the board pack a vanity project. With it, each tool is woven into practice, revisited, tested, and acted upon. The cadence is the spine, the habit that turns ideas into behaviour.

But rhythm carries its own challenge. Once the beat is set, it will expose discomfort: cash gaps, broken promises, underperforming metrics. The temptation will be to soften it, to skip weeks, to expand the agenda until sharpness dulls. The test of leadership is to resist that drift. For the discipline of one hour, once a week, is more than a meeting. It is a choice about how seriously you take control. The unanswered question is whether you will treat it as a ritual to endure, or as a lever to command.

Chapter 2
Cash Is a Drumbeat

In 1987, a Glasgow café owner found herself staring at an odd paradox. Her till overflowed with coins from a weekend rush, yet her supplier refused to extend more credit. She had milk, beans, and bread to buy on Monday morning, but her profits—impressive on paper—were locked up in unpaid tabs from regulars. Two streets away, an advertising agency thrived with barely any stock at all, its office filled with files rather than food. Yet that agency, too, struggled, waiting ninety days for clients to settle invoices while wages and rent drained the account. Both businesses, wildly different in form, were prisoners of the same truth: cash flow is not a matter of success or failure alone, but of timing, rhythm, and the choreography of working capital.

It is a mistake to think of cash as an abstract pool, static and stored. In practice, it moves like blood through arteries—too slow and the body weakens, too fast and the system strains. The café's problem lay in *inventory*: milk bought in bulk, bread wasted at the end of the day, beans purchased upfront. The agency's problem lay in *receivables*: invoices issued, promises made, yet cash withheld for weeks. Each had its own working capital trap, each demanding different levers to keep the rhythm steady. Businesses that fail to recognise these patterns often discover, too late, that survival is not about profit margins but about the ability to keep the beat.

Cash is not only a resource but a tempo. Unlike annual budgets or quarterly reports, which lull managers into thinking they have time, cash insists on immediacy. Payroll is due on Friday whether or not clients pay on Thursday. Suppliers demand terms whether or not sales match forecasts. The discipline lies in choosing a time horizon that is long enough to provide foresight but short enough to compel action. Thirteen weeks—one quarter—is the window that reconciles the two. It allows owners to see beyond the week-to-week scramble, but it is near enough that promises can be tested against reality. Beyond thirteen weeks, forecasts dissolve into fantasy. Within thirteen weeks, cash speaks with clarity.

But a forecast alone does not change behaviour. Too many founders build spreadsheets like cathedrals: elaborate, beautiful, yet disconnected from daily life. The power of the 13-week window lies not in its charts but in its conversations. Each week, the forecast should trigger three questions: What has changed since last week? What must we do differently now? What commitments will close the gaps? Numbers without action are decoration. Numbers tied to owners, deadlines, and certainty bands become levers. Confidence grows not from the model itself, but from the discipline of treating it as a living document—an agenda for decisions, not a monument to analysis.

The subtlety is in the signals. Cash itself lags; by the time the account dips, the danger has already arrived. Leading indicators—pipeline quality, time from proposal to acceptance, early signs of customer churn—move before the cash does. Monitoring them reduces surprise and creates space to act. A manufacturer, for instance, learns that a dip in order backlog predicts a cash crunch weeks before it shows up in the bank. A consultancy notices that when average proposal turnaround slows, collections will falter soon after. Each business must learn its own language of signals. Those who listen early can adjust course; those who wait for the bank balance are already too late.

To treat cash as a drumbeat is to accept that finance is not static reporting but living rhythm. It is the cadence that binds decisions week by week, the flow that sustains growth without collapse. A founder who grasps this truth begins to see working capital not as housekeeping but as strategy; forecasts not as spreadsheets but as commitments; metrics not as vanity but as motion.

The open question, of course, is whether you will hear the beat before it falters. If cash is rhythm, then silence is collapse. The pages ahead will not simply explain how to count the notes, but how to keep the tempo steady enough for everything else—the product, the people, the vision—to play on.

Working capital as strategy

In 2008, at the height of the financial crisis, a British retailer discovered that survival was not about revenue, profit, or even debt. It was about whether suppliers would keep delivering stock. Customers were still buying, shops were still full, but when the credit insurers pulled cover, wholesalers demanded cash on delivery. Overnight, the retailer's carefully negotiated thirty-day payment terms collapsed into zero. Within weeks, stores shuttered and thousands lost their jobs. The lesson was stark: working capital—those lines between what you hold, what you are owed, and what you must pay—is not a background detail of finance. It is the battlefield on which survival is won or lost.

Working capital is often described as the gap between current assets and current liabilities. That definition is accurate but bloodless. In practice, it is the choreography of three flows: inventory, receivables, and payables. Each line has its own rhythm. Inventory ties up cash in goods that may sit unsold. Receivables lock it in promises from customers who may delay. Payables dictate when you must part with it to suppliers. Together they determine how long cash stays trapped before it returns. This cycle, measured not in theory but in days, dictates whether a business runs lean and agile or bloated and brittle.

Three measures capture the truth with clarity. **Days Inventory Outstanding (DIO)** shows how long stock sits before it is sold. **Days Sales Outstanding (DSO)** measures how long it takes to collect from customers once sales are made. **Days Payables Outstanding (DPO)** captures how long you can delay paying suppliers. Each number is simple; the interplay is profound. Add DIO and DSO, subtract DPO, and you discover your *cash conversion cycle*:

the number of days your cash is tied up before it is freed again. Shorten the cycle, and you liberate working capital to fund growth or resilience. Lengthen it, and you starve your business even as sales climb.

Consider a café. Every morning it buys milk, beans, and bread. Inventory turns within days: coffee beans ground, milk steamed, sandwiches sold by lunchtime. Receivables are almost zero; customers pay at the counter. But payables are immediate too—suppliers often demand cash or very short terms. The café's cash cycle is brutally short: what comes in leaves almost as quickly. Liquidity depends on tightly matching daily inflows to daily outflows. The café owner's levers are obvious but limited: reduce waste, negotiate supplier terms, increase average ticket size. A day's slip in either direction can mean unpaid wages.

Now contrast the advertising agency down the street. It holds no inventory. Its product is hours of creative work. But its receivables are long; clients may take sixty or ninety days to pay. Payables, meanwhile, are inflexible: rent, salaries, and software subscriptions demand punctual cash. The agency's cash cycle stretches dangerously. Each new project amplifies the strain, as staff are paid monthly but invoices are settled quarterly. Unlike the café, the agency has only one lever of real power: receivables. It must accelerate client payments, demand deposits, or shift terms—or else it bleeds cash while showing paper profits.

The compounding effects of small changes are easy to underestimate. A manufacturer who reduces DIO by just five days—by selling stock faster—releases thousands in cash. A contractor who shortens DSO by a fortnight—by chasing invoices earlier or requiring partial upfront payments—may save enough to fund a new hire without external finance. Conversely, if suppliers tighten DPO by ten days, the impact can be catastrophic, forcing businesses to bridge the gap with overdrafts or equity. Working capital shifts are rarely dramatic on paper, but in practice they are seismic, because they ripple across every transaction and accumulate over time.

To treat working capital as strategy is to recognise that these levers are not housekeeping but power. A founder negotiating supplier terms is not just haggling over days; they are shaping the liquidity of the enterprise. A sales director who insists on upfront deposits is not being awkward; they are securing the firm's survival. Every decision—when to order, when to bill, when to pay—is a decision about cash tempo. Companies that ignore this relegate themselves to financial fragility, perpetually reliant on overdrafts or outside capital. Those that master it can finance growth from within, turning operational discipline into competitive strength.

Behavioural blind spots often stand in the way. Managers are rewarded for revenue and profit, rarely for cash cycle efficiency. Sales teams celebrate big wins even if the client pays glacially. Operations teams hoard inventory "just in case," tying up cash in warehouses. Finance teams, meanwhile, present figures retrospectively, long after the damage is done. To break the cycle, leadership must reframe incentives: measuring not only what is sold but how fast it converts to cash.

History offers striking lessons. Toyota revolutionised global manufacturing not simply by building cars cheaply but by mastering inventory discipline. Just-in-time production reduced DIO to a fraction of its competitors, liberating capital and enabling reinvestment in innovation. Conversely, during the dot-com bubble, countless start-ups collapsed not because demand was absent but because their receivables ballooned beyond control. They were owed millions yet had nothing to pay salaries. In both cases, working capital management—not strategy decks or marketing slogans—decided survival.

Philosophically, working capital exposes a deeper truth: value is not realised until it returns as cash. Until then, it is promise, not power. Businesses often confuse activity with liquidity—sales booked, goods shipped, contracts signed. But until those flows complete, cash is absent. Working capital is the discipline of seeing through illusion to reality, of recognising that every pound tied up in stock or invoices is a pound unavailable for payroll, investment, or resilience.

The unresolved question is not whether working capital matters—it always has, and always will—but whether leaders will treat it with the seriousness of strategy rather than the tedium of accounting. Will you see inventory, receivables, and payables as passive lines on a balance sheet, or as levers to be pulled with precision? The answer will shape whether your business is perpetually scrambling for oxygen or breathing steadily enough to grow.

The 13-week window

In 1979, Chrysler was on the brink of collapse. Revenues were high, and the company still posted profits on paper, but cash had evaporated. Factories kept running, suppliers demanded payment, and banks closed their doors. What saved the firm in the short term was not an elaborate turnaround plan but a brutally simple discipline: weekly visibility over the next thirteen weeks of cash. The management team abandoned annual projections and five-year visions and instead focused relentlessly on the near horizon—just long enough to matter, just short enough to control. The lesson is timeless: survival is decided not in theory but in the rhythm of weeks.

Business owners often fall into one of two traps. Some bury themselves in short-term firefighting, reacting to daily bank balances, convinced that if today's bills are paid, tomorrow will somehow solve itself. Others retreat into long-range plans, filled with colour-coded charts and lofty assumptions, convinced that detail confers control. Both approaches fail. The first breeds exhaustion; the second breeds delusion. The 13-week window avoids both extremes. It recognises that thirteen weeks—a quarter—is the right span: it gives enough distance to see trouble forming, yet remains close enough that promises can be tested against reality.

The strength of the window lies in its simplicity. Its inputs are modest: opening cash, expected inflows, committed outflows. Rent, wages, supplier bills, tax, loan repayments. Customer payments mapped not by wishful due dates but by likely clearance dates. Precision is avoided; false accuracy is the enemy. A forecast that pretends to know the exact value of receipts in week eleven is a work of fiction. What matters is not decimal places but order of magnitude: will the business run dry, and if so, when? The 13-week view sharpens foresight without falling into fantasy.

When used properly, the model forces three weekly conversations that cut deeper than any report. First: *What has changed since last week?* Cash is reconciled against forecast, and variances are interrogated. A payment arrived late, a supplier granted an extension, sales slipped by 10%. These differences matter less as judgements and more as information. Second: *What must we do differently now?* If the forecast shows a gap, what action will close it—collect faster, defer a cost, renegotiate terms? Third: *What commitments will we make this week?* Without owners and deadlines, forecasts are ornamental. With them, they become levers.

A consultancy in Edinburgh illustrates the point. For years it relied on annual budgets produced each January, dutifully filed and largely ignored. Mid-year cash shortages were met with panic overdrafts and staff pay deferrals. When it adopted a 13-week forecast, the effect was immediate. The model showed that despite rising sales, cash would collapse in week eight due to staggered client payments. By week three, they had adjusted invoicing terms, secured deposits, and avoided the crisis entirely. Nothing in their profit and loss statement had changed; only the horizon had.

The temptation for many is to begin in spreadsheets. But the real discipline begins with paper. A simple table sketched by hand—cash in, cash out, balance remaining—forces clarity. On paper, optimism is harder to disguise. Once the shape is clear, a spreadsheet can add rigour, but only as a servant, not a master. The essence lies in the conversation, not the formatting.

Philosophically, the 13-week window is more than a tool. It is a recognition of human limits. We are poor at imagining distant futures; optimism and abstraction blur the truth. Thirteen weeks is close enough to be concrete—payroll dates, invoices due, contracts to be signed—yet far enough to demand foresight. It turns finance from a retrospective language into a predictive one. It changes time itself from something that happens to you into something you manage.

Yet the discipline is uncomfortable. The forecast will expose unpleasant truths: that a celebrated contract will not produce cash for two months, that payroll commitments outstrip likely inflows, that growth itself is unsustainable without adjustment. Many founders prefer the comfort of profit figures or the distraction of long-term plans. The 13-week horizon strips away those illusions. It asks not whether your business looks healthy on paper, but whether it can breathe through the quarter ahead.

And so the open question lingers: if survival depends on the rhythm of weeks, why would any leader look only at months or years? To embrace the 13-week window is to accept that control is not abstract but immediate, that foresight is not luxury but necessity. The choice, ultimately, is stark: will you step into the discipline of thirteen weeks, or will you trust that the future will bend itself to your plans?

From forecast to behaviour

In the late 1990s, a well-known retailer collapsed with shelves still stocked and profits still reported. Analysts were baffled: how could a company that seemed solvent on paper unravel so quickly? The truth, discovered in the aftermath, was stark. The firm had no discipline of ownership over its forecasts. Numbers were produced, but no one was accountable for them. Charts were built, but no one translated them into action. Forecasts became theatre—convincing to watch, useless in practice. What should have been a living instrument for steering the business had calcified into static reports.

This is the paradox of forecasting: it is not the spreadsheet that saves you, but the behaviour it provokes. Many firms mistake forecast accuracy for control, as if precision itself were the goal. But a forecast without ownership is little more than numerology. Cash flow is not improved by beautiful graphs; it is improved by phone calls, renegotiations, deferred expenses, accelerated billings—each tied to specific people, deadlines, and commitments. The discipline is not in the chart but in the chain of responsibility it creates.

The first step is to bind each line item to an owner. If £20,000 is expected from Client A in week six, who will ensure the invoice is chased, the payment confirmed, the funds cleared? If payroll of £15,000 is due in week four, who owns the responsibility of ensuring cash is ready? Without ownership, line items are abstractions—someone else's problem, no one's priority. Ownership converts numbers into obligations. It also reveals bottlenecks: if too many critical lines depend on the same person, capacity is stretched, and risk is exposed.

Deadlines sharpen the effect. A forecast that predicts receipts "sometime next month" is useless; one that states "by Friday, 12th May" compels action. Humans respond to immediacy. A sales manager asked to collect an invoice within three weeks may delay; one asked to secure it by next Friday will make the call today. Specificity removes ambiguity, and ambiguity is the enemy of accountability. The beauty of the 13-week horizon is that it makes deadlines concrete: not vague quarters or fiscal years, but named Fridays that approach relentlessly.

Uncertainty, however, must be acknowledged. No forecast is certain, and pretending otherwise leads to disappointment and blame. The antidote is to tag entries with confidence bands. Some inflows are near-guaranteed: standing orders, long-standing clients with punctual habits. Others are less certain: a new customer still within cooling-off, a supplier rebate promised but not yet documented. Labelling each entry as high, medium, or low confidence does not weaken the forecast; it strengthens it. It reframes the model from false precision into probabilistic awareness. Leaders can then plan contingencies, rather than reacting with shock when "expected" cash fails to arrive.

This probabilistic view also humanises forecasting. Teams stop arguing about who was "wrong" and instead discuss levels of certainty. Optimists still project best-case scenarios, but pessimists can temper them with confidence bands. Over time, the business learns from its own biases: are sales managers consistently over-optimistic? Do finance teams underestimate delays? Each forecast becomes not just a projection but a feedback loop, refining the organisation's judgement week by week.

Case studies make the difference clear. A London-based software company once built quarterly forecasts showing surging inflows from enterprise clients. In reality, procurement delays meant payments arrived months late. The result: profitable growth paired with a cash crisis. When the firm switched to binding line items with owners and confidence bands, the conversation changed. Inflows were no longer passive numbers but active tasks: "James to follow up with procurement director on Tuesday." Each week, variance between forecast and actual was discussed, and biases were adjusted. Within two quarters, cash stabilised—not because sales grew faster, but because commitments were treated as levers rather than assumptions.

The philosophical point here is that forecasts are not predictions but instruments of coordination. They are less about knowing the future than about organising the present. A forecast that compels conversation and action is valuable even if "wrong" in detail. A forecast that exists merely as a chart is worthless even if numerically accurate. The distinction is subtle but decisive: forecasts should be judged not by their precision but by the behaviours they trigger.

Sketching forecasts on paper before transposing them into spreadsheets helps preserve this truth. Paper forces brevity; it reveals structure without ornamentation. On paper, each line can be interrogated: *Who owns this? How confident are we? What must be done?* In spreadsheets, detail often overwhelms, leading to false confidence. By starting simple, the focus remains on behaviour. The spreadsheet becomes a servant, not a master.

Each week, the living list must advance. Forecasts are not static artefacts to be filed and forgotten; they are rolling agendas. The list should shrink and shift as actions are completed, inflows arrive, and new commitments are made. A healthy forecast is in motion, evolving as the business evolves. When owners treat it this way, the forecast ceases to be a chore. It becomes a mirror of reality, a prompt for decisions, a guardrail against drift.

But there is an unresolved tension. Most leaders want certainty where none exists. They crave the reassurance of numbers that promise control. Yet the true power of forecasting lies not in certainty but in confronting uncertainty—naming it, owning it, acting in spite of it. The question, then, is whether you will treat your forecast as a chart to display, or as a discipline to live by. The answer determines not only how accurate your numbers appear, but whether your business has the resilience to endure the weeks ahead.

Leading vs lagging cash signals

When the collapse of Carillion shook Britain in 2018, the headlines spoke of a sudden implosion. In truth, the warning signs had been visible for years. Contracts were delayed, invoices contested, projects running over schedule. Yet the company's reported profits continued to appear healthy until the very end. By the time the cash position revealed the rot, it was too late. The failure was not merely financial but diagnostic: the firm mistook lagging signals for leading ones, preferring the comfort of historic numbers over the discomfort of early warnings.

This is the central paradox of cash management: by the time cash flow confirms a problem, the problem has already matured. Cash is the most objective measure, but it is also the slowest to speak. Waiting for the bank balance to tell you the truth is like waiting for a fever to break before acknowledging an infection. The discipline lies in cultivating earlier signals—indicators that move before cash does, providing the foresight to act while there is still time.

The distinction between leading and lagging signals is deceptively simple. Lagging signals tell you what has already happened: sales booked, cash collected, bills paid. They are reliable, but retrospective. Leading signals, by contrast, hint at what is to come: the strength of your pipeline, the speed of your proposals, the acceptance of your invoices. They are less certain but infinitely more useful. A business that trains itself to listen to these anticipatory whispers can reduce the shock of sudden crises.

Consider pipeline quality. A consultancy with a dozen strong leads may feel confident, but the true signal lies in the conversion ratio and the velocity through stages. If proposals are stalling in procurement, cash will stall weeks later. If win rates slip by ten percent, the shortfall will echo in collections long after. Monitoring pipeline depth without examining movement is like weighing food without checking whether it is edible. The velocity and conversion of opportunities are the true harbingers of cash health.

Proposal-to-win time is another powerful indicator. In industries where contracts involve negotiation, the lag between proposal submission and client signature often predicts cash inflows more accurately than sales forecasts. If the average time creeps upward—from, say, three weeks to six—future inflows are silently receding. The business may still celebrate "pipeline growth" while failing to see that momentum has slowed. A disciplined firm treats proposal-to-win time as a pressure gauge: when it lengthens, something in the system needs adjustment—pricing, terms, responsiveness, or client targeting.

Invoice acceptance may appear mundane, but it is one of the most overlooked early warnings. An invoice not formally accepted is an invoice not yet collectable. Too many businesses mistake "invoice issued" for "cash imminent." In reality, disputes, formatting errors, or slow approvals can delay payments by weeks. Firms that track acceptance as a distinct stage—separate from issuance—gain visibility over the bottleneck. A manufacturing company in Birmingham once discovered that its average time from invoice to acceptance was twenty-one days. By resolving this gap—through clearer purchase order matching and proactive follow-ups—it shortened its overall cash cycle more than any discounting scheme could achieve.

Different business models demand different leading signals. For a café, footfall and daily ticket size are more predictive than accounts receivable, because cash is immediate and the warning signs lie in customer behaviour. For an agency, client pipeline and contract negotiations are the heartbeat, since payments lag by months. For a manufacturer, order backlog and supplier lead times offer better foresight than cash on hand. There is no universal dashboard; the art lies in selecting the signals that truly precede cash for your model.

Philosophically, the challenge is that humans prefer lagging signals. They are clean, confirmed, unambiguous. Leading signals are messy, probabilistic, and subject to interpretation. Yet leadership requires tolerating ambiguity in exchange for foresight. It requires the humility to accept that early warnings will sometimes prove false alarms, but that the cost of listening is far lower than the cost of blindness. A pilot ignores the first hint of turbulence at their peril. A business leader who ignores slowing proposals or delayed invoice acceptances courts the same fate.

The discipline, then, is not only technical but cultural. It requires creating an environment where leading signals are discussed weekly, not dismissed as "soft data." It demands that teams treat small shifts as worthy of attention, not as noise to be rationalised away. Over time, this vigilance builds a radar that can detect storms long before they appear on the cash statement.

Yet the question remains unresolved: will leaders choose the comfort of certainty or the discomfort of foresight? Cash itself is the final truth, but it is a truth that arrives late. The test of resilience lies in whether a business can act on the murmurs that precede it—the subtle changes in pipeline, proposals, and approvals—before the silence of an empty bank account forces the lesson home.

Chapter 3
Unit Economics That Decide Survival

In 2012, a boutique gym in Manchester celebrated record sign-ups. Membership cards were flying out the door, revenue charts pointed upward, and the owner assumed profitability was all but guaranteed. Yet by year's end, the gym was drowning in debt. The paradox lay hidden in its unit economics. The business had priced memberships by month but measured costs per class. The mismatch meant that heavily used memberships were loss-making, subsidised by casual attenders. The "average" revenue figure looked healthy, but when the unit was properly defined—class attended versus seat sold—it became clear that each popular spin session was costing money rather than making it. Growth had not saved the business; it had hastened its collapse.

Stories like this repeat across industries. A restaurant that thinks in terms of covers rather than tables misses that dwell time, not diners, dictates revenue. A software-as-a-service company that trumpets gross revenue while ignoring contribution per user discovers too late that customer acquisition costs never pay back. A contractor who celebrates a large project win realises only afterwards that true variable costs—overtime, outsourced labour, equipment hire—erased the margin entirely. Businesses don't usually collapse because they lack ambition. They collapse because they scale without clarity on what unit sustains them.

This chapter takes aim at the deceptively simple question: *what is the unit that pays your rent?* Define it poorly, and you will manage on illusions. Define it well, and you gain the lens through which all other decisions—pricing, cost control, growth strategy—become sharper. The unit is not always obvious. For a gym, is it a member, a class, or a month? For a café, is it a coffee sold, a customer served, or an hour of table time? For a software company, is it a subscription, a login, or an active user? The choice changes comparability, changes pricing power, and can expose losses that topline revenue conceals.

Yet even with the right unit, survival rests not on gross numbers but on contribution. A founder dazzled by turnover often forgets that not all revenue is created equal. A £10,000 contract that absorbs £9,500 in variable costs adds little to survival. A smaller £4,000 deal with £1,000 in true variable costs may contribute more, pound for pound, to the business's endurance. Contribution per unit—and, crucially, per constrained resource, whether hours of staff time, machine capacity, or square footage—reveals where profit is actually made. A quick constraint analysis often flips priorities upside down: the "biggest" client may be the least valuable, the "minor" service line the one that keeps the lights on.

Subscription and repeat-purchase businesses face their own test: payback. It is not enough to boast of "lifetime value" inflated by hypothetical upsell. The honest measure is how many billing cycles it takes to recover the cost of acquiring a customer. A company that needs twelve months to break even but retains clients for only nine is effectively eating its own capital. Yet tighten payback by even a single cycle—say, from six months to five—and the same business can fund growth from its own operations. Retention, too, ceases to be a marketing slogan and becomes a cash decision: every extra month a customer stays is liquidity preserved.

Perhaps the most underused tool in unit economics is sensitivity analysis. The slope of a line matters more than the size of a cost base. A £1 increase in price, a 1% change in churn, or a 5% rise in utilisation can outweigh months of belt-tightening. Ranking these slope lines by impact focuses attention on the moves that truly bend survival odds. This perspective replaces generic cost-cutting—sack staff, trim expenses—with targeted levers: change price here, renegotiate terms there, redesign utilisation of a bottleneck resource. A dashboard that is slope-aware is not just descriptive but prescriptive.

The intellectual stakes are high. Unit economics is not bookkeeping; it is the grammar of survival. It forces leaders to strip away vanity metrics and reckon with the mechanics of how value is created, sustained, and converted back into cash. For centuries, merchants measured their ventures by voyages, not by individual trades—because they understood that only when a ship returned to port laden with goods did profit exist. Today's founders face the same discipline. The unit may be digital, the horizon shorter, but the principle is unchanged: survival depends not on stories told to investors or headlines in reports but on the economics of the unit that keeps the doors open.

The unanswered question is whether leaders will take this lens seriously before reality forces it upon them. Will they probe beneath revenue headlines to discover the unit that truly sustains their business? Or will they mistake growth for health, and discover too late that scaling an unhealthy unit only accelerates decline? The pages that follow offer not comfort but clarity—a set of tools to expose the truth and levers to act on it. For in the end, it is not ambition or vision that decides survival, but whether your unit economics make growth a gift or a poison.

Define the unit that pays the rent

In 2012, a small but ambitious independent gym in Manchester proudly announced that it had doubled its membership. To outsiders, the growth looked like success incarnate: rows of treadmills buzzing with activity, classes oversubscribed, lockers filled with paying customers. Yet behind the reception desk, the numbers told a darker story. Despite the influx of members, the gym was bleeding cash. The problem was not footfall but framing. Management measured success by the *month-long membership* but overlooked the true economic unit that drove costs: *the class attended*. Heavy users—those turning up five or six times a week—were effectively subsidised by casual members who rarely set foot inside. Growth magnified this distortion. Each new sign-up added revenue, yes, but every enthusiast who actually used the service ate into the gym's margins.

By defining the wrong unit, the owners were celebrating their own destruction.

The paradox is common. Businesses cling to "average" metrics that conceal more than they reveal. A restaurant may count covers but ignore the length of table occupation. A software start-up may track subscriptions without distinguishing between active and inactive users. An architecture practice may tally projects, treating each as equivalent, though one ties up staff for six months while another turns around in two weeks. Without a precise definition of the unit that *pays the rent*, the story managers tell themselves—and their investors—drifts further and further from reality.

The question, then, is deceptively simple: what is your economic unit? An order? A seat? A project? A month? The answer dictates not only how you measure performance but how you wield pricing power and judge comparability. For a café, a "cup of coffee sold" may seem the obvious unit. Yet if peak hours are the true bottleneck, then the more meaningful measure is revenue per seat-hour, not per cup. If you run a theatre, a seat is a natural unit—but the distinction between sold-out weekends and empty midweeks is decisive. For a consultancy, the project is the unit, but capacity is finite; a single overextended client may cannibalise opportunities for several smaller, more profitable ones.

Choosing the wrong unit creates illusions of strength. Consider two gyms: Gym A charges £50 a month for unlimited access, Gym B charges £5 per class. Gym A boasts of 1,000 members, while Gym B manages only 400 regular attendees. On paper, Gym A is "larger". Yet if the majority of Gym A's members attend four or more classes a week, each workout is generating barely £3 in revenue, far less than the £5 charged by Gym B. Once staffing, equipment, and heating costs are factored in, Gym A may be losing money on its most dedicated customers, whereas Gym B maintains positive contribution margins class by class. The key difference is not operational excellence but the unit each gym has chosen to measure and manage.

This is why comparability matters. Investors, lenders, even managers themselves often mislead when they standardise metrics across industries without respecting unit differences. Comparing revenue per "customer" across a subscription software company and a café is meaningless unless we define whether that "customer" refers to a monthly subscriber, a daily visitor, or an annual contract. By standardising the unit within a given business—choosing one consistent frame of analysis—you create clarity for internal decision-making and comparability across time. Without that, dashboards devolve into chaos: each department reporting numbers that cannot be reconciled, each function celebrating a different story.

Philosophically, this question cuts deeper. The act of defining a unit is not merely technical—it shapes behaviour. If staff know they are judged by "tables turned", they will hurry diners. If they are judged by "customer spend per visit", they will upsell desserts. If they are judged by "subscriptions sold", they will chase sign-ups regardless of whether those customers churn in a month. Measurement defines motivation; the unit becomes the lens through which survival is sought. To ignore this is to confuse movement with progress.

It is tempting to think that one can postpone such precision until the business is larger, but this is a costly illusion. Small businesses, with thinner buffers, suffer more acutely from mismeasured units. A gym with fifty members cannot afford to misprice classes for even a month; the cash bleed is immediate. A café that defines its unit wrongly may find peak-hour queues masking the fact that evening trade cannot cover fixed rent. To define the economic unit early is to give yourself a compass before the storm gathers.

Yet clarity does not mean simplicity. The correct unit is often counterintuitive. A subscription streaming service, for example, might assume the month is the unit. But when licensing costs scale with the number of streams, the true unit is not the subscriber but the *hour of content consumed*. Suddenly, the binge-watcher is no longer a prized customer but a cost centre. Such revelations can feel uncomfortable, even disloyal to the intuition that "a customer is always good news". But to see reality clearly is the first duty of survival.

So, what should the business leader do? The task is to standardise the unit, not because it offers comfort but because it strips away self-deception. Define it precisely, test its assumptions, and then use it consistently. Only then do comparisons across months or product lines reveal truth rather than noise. The exercise may feel sterile, but the stakes are existential. One can scale indefinitely on illusions—until, as with the Manchester gym, the cash runs dry.

The unanswered tension remains: how many businesses today are operating on false units, congratulating themselves on growth that is hollow? How many gyms, cafés, agencies, and software start-ups will discover too late that their chosen unit was the wrong one? Defining the unit that pays the rent is less a technical choice than a moral one: are you willing to look your business in the eye and ask what truly sustains it? And if you find the answer uncomfortable, will you have the courage to act on it?

Contribution, not gross, runs the show

In 1982, a small family-owned bakery in Yorkshire found itself in a dilemma. Every Saturday, customers queued down the street for its famed iced buns. The owners, encouraged by the rush, assumed the buns were their most profitable item. After all, each tray brought in more cash than loaves of bread, which sold at steadier, slower rates. When a local accountant finally examined their books, the truth was humbling. Once butter, icing sugar, and additional labour hours were allocated, the buns delivered barely a fraction of the bakery's *contribution*—the surplus left after variable costs—compared to the humble loaf. Worse, the buns monopolised the oven during peak hours, displacing the steady sellers that actually kept the business afloat. What looked like a star product was, in fact, a parasite.

This story is not about bread. It is about the widespread illusion that gross margin is enough to judge performance. Managers who lean on gross profit often mistake volume for value, applauding products or clients that "grow revenue" while quietly eroding the very oxygen of survival: contribution. Gross measures include costs that do not scale directly with each unit sold—rents, salaries, shared marketing overheads—masking the true economics of incremental sales. Contribution, by contrast, is brutally honest: price minus all costs that rise with that unit. It answers the fundamental question, *if I sell one more, what do I really gain?*

This distinction matters most in constrained systems, which is to say, in all real businesses. A factory line can only produce so many units per shift, a consultancy so many billable hours per month, a café so many tables at once. If a product eats scarce capacity while yielding low contribution, it quietly destroys value—even if gross margins look respectable. This is why contribution per *constrained hour* often matters more than contribution per unit. The bakery could not bake everything its customers wanted. Its oven was the bottleneck. Every bun displaced loaves that would have generated more contribution per oven-hour. The apparent bestseller was cannibalising survival.

The idea is simple enough, yet businesses fall into the trap repeatedly. Airlines once pursued "load factor"—the percentage of seats filled—assuming a fuller plane meant greater profit. But filling a plane with discount tickets often yielded less contribution than leaving seats empty and preserving pricing integrity. Tech companies trumpet user numbers while ignoring the incremental costs of serving "free" or low-paying customers—support queries, server loads, licensing fees. Consultancies chase prestige projects at marquee clients, overlooking that the additional travel and senior partner hours consume scarce attention that could have been spread across multiple smaller, higher-contribution contracts. Gross blinds; contribution reveals.

To apply this lens requires discipline in separating true variable costs from everything else. Many managers are sloppy here, misclassifying semi-fixed expenses as "variable" simply because they vary somewhat. The test is simple: *does this cost rise directly with one more unit sold?* Raw ingredients, shipping, commission payments—yes. Rent, insurance, salaried staff—no. Even "grey" areas like utilities or consumables can usually be apportioned with reasonable accuracy. Once this clarity is established, contribution analysis stops being an abstract formula and becomes a practical steering wheel.

From there, constraint analysis adds the necessary dimension of realism. It is not enough to know contribution per unit; one must ask, *what limits the system?* In many service businesses, the scarcest resource is not cash but time:

billable hours of skilled staff. A law firm may have dozens of potential clients but only so many associates and partners to handle cases. If one client consumes an outsized number of hours for modest contribution, that client is more damaging than their gross invoice suggests. In manufacturing, the constraint might be machine uptime; in logistics, vehicle availability; in software, server bandwidth or developer focus. Whatever the bottleneck, contribution should be calculated per unit of it. Price not against the illusion of "per customer" but against the reality of what each scarce hour or unit of capacity returns.

There is also a philosophical dimension here. To manage by gross margin is to indulge in abstraction, to comfort oneself with averages. To manage by contribution is to face reality at its sharpest edge: what does each marginal action deliver? It is a move from theory to agency, from the rear-view mirror to the steering wheel. In human terms, it asks: are we rewarding ourselves for busyness, or for progress? Are we filling the oven with buns because the queue looks impressive, or because it keeps the lights on?

The discipline of contribution analysis can be sobering. Many cherished products, beloved clients, or legacy services turn out to be quietly harmful once costs and constraints are measured honestly. The temptation is to explain them away as "strategic investments" or "loss leaders". But unless they feed into a credible path toward future contribution, they are often rationalised losses. The baker might tell himself the buns "bring people in" who then buy loaves—but the evidence must be tested, not assumed. Otherwise, the business remains captive to sentiment rather than survival.

The unresolved tension is this: how many organisations today are still running their ovens full of iced buns? How many leaders comfort themselves with gross margins while ignoring contribution per scarce hour? To face this honestly may mean repricing, restructuring, even shedding entire product lines or clients. Yet the alternative is worse: to drift on illusions until the constraint forces the truth upon

Cohort and payback logic

The paradox of modern growth stories is that some of the fastest-growing companies are also the most fragile. It is not uncommon to find a start-up lauded for tripling revenue in a year while quietly bleeding cash to the point of collapse. At the heart of this contradiction lies a simple but often ignored truth: growth is only sustainable when the cost of acquiring a customer is repaid swiftly, and the retention of that customer generates real—not theoretical—value. Strip away the marketing gloss, and every business lives or dies on its payback logic.

Consider a subscription-based gym. It celebrates a surge of new sign-ups each January, fuelled by resolution-driven enthusiasm. On paper, revenue spikes. But if most of those members vanish before Easter, the apparent success masks a structural weakness. The gym may convince itself that upsells—personal training packages or merchandise—will fill the gap. Yet those are speculative promises, not cash in hand. Unless the basic subscription pays back its acquisition cost quickly, and members stay long enough to cover the churn, the business is subsidising failure.

This is why the notion of *cohorts* matters so deeply. A cohort is not an abstraction; it is a lived group of customers who signed up at a particular time, each carrying a story of commitment or abandonment. Tracking them honestly—month by month—reveals patterns of survival that averages obscure. An overall churn rate of 5% might sound tolerable until you realise that the January cohort is vanishing at twice the rate of the June one. Aggregated data soothes; cohort data unsettles. But only the latter tells you whether you are compounding strength or quietly eroding it.

At the centre of this analysis lies the payback period: the length of time it takes to recover the cost of acquiring a customer. Imagine you spend £100 to gain a subscriber who pays £20 a month. If they stay for six months, you break even. If they leave after three, you have lost £40. Every business has its own numbers, but the principle holds universally: the shorter the payback, the more resilient the model. The elegance of the metric lies in its concreteness—it converts vague hopes about "lifetime value" into a countdown clock visible to all.

Yet many companies prefer to lean on lifetime value, or LTV, as their comfort blanket. By projecting years of expected revenue, they inflate the apparent worth of each customer. A SaaS business might boast that each client is worth £1,000 over five years, but if those projections assume a best-case scenario of zero churn and constant upsell, they are fantasies rather than forecasts. Honest LTV requires brutal realism: strip away wishful thinking, exclude speculative upsells, and test the durability of retention. In many cases, the revised figure is half—or less—of the marketing slide.

The true power of payback logic emerges when you make retention a cash decision. Instead of treating customer loyalty as a fuzzy brand outcome, you quantify it in weeks of runway and months of survival. If you can shave a billing cycle from the payback horizon—recovering costs in four months instead of five—you may unlock growth without external funding. The compounding effect is profound: a business that funds its own expansion through disciplined payback cycles controls its destiny, while one that relies on capital injections is perpetually beholden to others.

Subscription businesses are the most obvious laboratory for this principle, but it applies equally to repeat-purchase models. A coffee shop may think less in terms of churn than in terms of visit frequency. If it costs £5 to attract a new customer who spends £3 per visit, payback depends on whether they return for a second cup, and how quickly. An e-commerce company selling consumables faces the same question: how many repeat orders are required to recover the first click's cost? In both cases, accelerating payback—through loyalty nudges, bundles, or subscription offers—transforms cash flow.

Philosophically, cohort and payback logic remind us that the present cannot be postponed indefinitely. Businesses are prone to promising themselves that tomorrow's upsell will justify today's deficit, or that growth will somehow outrun fragility. Yet the arithmetic of cash demands immediacy. By tethering your analysis to actual cohorts, and calculating payback with honesty, you strip away the illusions that so often fuel overconfidence. It is a discipline that feels constraining at first—like a drumbeat that narrows your freedom. But in reality, it liberates: you stop pretending and start acting on truths.

What emerges is a more sober but more empowering strategy. Instead of asking "How much could a customer be worth in five years?" you ask "How quickly does this customer repay their cost today?" Instead of obsessing over abstract averages, you learn to watch specific groups as they reveal your strengths and weaknesses in real time. Instead of chasing growth for its own sake, you orient your business around the rhythm of survival and renewal.

And yet a tension remains. What happens when your industry rewards narratives of endless growth, while your own numbers tell you to slow down until payback tightens? Do you chase the valuation that investors demand, or the cash discipline that survival requires? This tension is not theoretical—it has broken companies that seemed untouchable. The real challenge is whether you have the courage to listen to your cohorts and respect the clock of payback. That decision, more than any pitch deck, determines whether your growth story is durable or destined to unravel.

Sensitivity lines

One of the most dangerous illusions in business is the belief that all improvements are created equal. Managers announce cost-cutting drives, optimise processes, or squeeze suppliers, assuming that every incremental effort contributes in the same way. Yet the reality is brutally uneven. A £1 increase in price, a 1% reduction in churn, or a 5% rise in utilisation can transform the economics of a company far more dramatically than months of belt-tightening. The problem is that few leaders have the discipline—or the courage—to map these differences. They scatter attention across dozens of initiatives when the truth is that only a handful of levers really matter.

Imagine two gyms standing on opposite sides of the same street. Both employ the same trainers, rent similar facilities, and charge roughly the same membership fees. One chooses to focus obsessively on reducing overheads—switching cleaning contractors, renegotiating utility bills, and trimming advertising spend. The other identifies that increasing membership fees by just £1 per week, coupled with a modest investment in customer experience to support the change, shifts its contribution margin by tens of thousands of pounds annually. The first gym saves pennies; the second alters its slope of survival. The lesson is stark: without understanding sensitivity lines, businesses misallocate their finite energy.

Sensitivity analysis is not an abstract exercise; it is a way of seeing the world. Every variable in your model has a slope—a measure of how changes in that variable affect your outcome. Price, churn, utilisation, and cost all slope differently. Some are steep, meaning small changes have outsized impact. Others are shallow, where significant effort yields little effect. To act without mapping these slopes is to walk blindfolded across uneven terrain, never knowing whether the next step leads uphill, downhill, or into a ditch.

The gym example makes this concrete, but it applies universally. A SaaS business, for instance, might discover that reducing churn by one percentage point increases lifetime value by more than doubling marketing spend. An airline may find that a single percentage improvement in seat utilisation creates more profit than negotiating fuel discounts that took a year to secure. A manufacturing company might realise that pricing discipline on its flagship product shifts margins far more than shaving costs on auxiliary lines. Sensitivity lines reveal where the hidden cliffs and gentle plains of your financial landscape lie.

Yet mapping sensitivity requires intellectual honesty and a tolerance for discomfort. Many organisations prefer the ritual of across-the-board cost control because it feels egalitarian and avoids conflict. Raising prices, by contrast, invites fear of customer backlash. Confronting churn demands that leaders acknowledge product or service weaknesses. Tackling utilisation means addressing scheduling inefficiencies or staff morale. The slopes that matter most are often the ones that provoke the greatest resistance. But ignoring them does not flatten the terrain; it simply ensures that you keep marching in the wrong direction.

The discipline of ranking slopes is what transforms sensitivity analysis from theory into practice. Once you have mapped the impact of each lever—£1 of price, 1% churn, 5% utilisation—you must order them ruthlessly. Which slope is steepest? Which variable is most responsive? This ranking becomes the heartbeat of your dashboard, the lens through which you interpret every meeting and decision. It prevents the diffusion of attention that kills so many small businesses, ensuring that scarce time and energy are concentrated where the slope is steep and the payoff swift.

There is also a deeper philosophical insight here. Sensitivity lines remind us that businesses are not democracies of effort; they are hierarchies of effect. It may feel more comfortable to spread attention evenly, but reality is lopsided. The disproportionate nature of cause and consequence echoes throughout human life—small habits compound into transformative change, while grand gestures often fade into irrelevance. In finance, as in life, not all levers are equal. Recognising and embracing this asymmetry is what separates leaders from administrators.

The dashboard, then, must evolve beyond a static set of numbers into a slope-aware instrument. Instead of celebrating superficial wins—a minor cost saving here, a negligible efficiency there—it should highlight the slope-adjusted impact of changes. When leaders see that a £1 price increase outpaces a 10% cut in stationery costs by orders of magnitude, they stop wasting breath on trivialities. When they grasp that tightening retention by a single billing cycle funds expansion more effectively than any loan, they begin to act with clarity. A slope-aware dashboard does not merely report; it teaches where to push and where to stop pretending.

Still, one challenge lingers. Knowing the steepest slope does not guarantee the will to act upon it. Raising prices may terrify a founder who equates growth with volume. Confronting churn may require admitting that customer experience is failing. Adjusting utilisation may disrupt entrenched schedules and hierarchies. Sensitivity lines illuminate the truth, but they do not erase human fear. The final leap is not analytical but moral: will you act on what the slopes reveal, or retreat into the safety of cosmetic changes?

The slopes are there whether you acknowledge them or not. They do not bend to your preferences or hide behind averages. They define the physics of your business, waiting to be measured and ranked. The real question is whether you will have the courage to make your strategy slope-aware—or whether you will continue scattering effort across shallow plains while the steep cliffs of survival and growth remain untouched.

Chapter 4
Pricing for Margin, Not Vanity

There is a peculiar silence that often fills a room when the subject of pricing arises. Entrepreneurs who will gladly debate marketing strategy or product features for hours suddenly become hesitant, defensive, or evasive when asked, *"Why do you charge what you charge?"* The answer is too often circular: "Because that's what the market pays," or "Because that's what competitors charge." Yet the market does not set your survival costs, nor do competitors pay your staff. The uncomfortable truth is that most businesses are not underpriced by their customers; they are underpriced by their own fear.

History offers reminders of this dynamic. When Henry Heinz first bottled ketchup in the late nineteenth century, rivals competed to undercut him, racing towards cheaper formulas and thinner margins. Heinz took the opposite path. He anchored his price to purity and consistency, investing in glass bottles that revealed the product's integrity. Customers were willing to pay more because the value was clear and visible. What looked like audacity—charging above the going rate—was in fact survival logic. Heinz built not just a product but a margin fortress. Fear pushes prices down; value lifts them up.

This chapter turns that silence into speech. It argues that pricing is not a matter of vanity metrics—boastful revenue figures, discount-driven spikes in sales, or a hollow "market share." It is the most powerful lever of financial health. A pound added to price flows directly to margin in ways that no cost-cutting initiative can match. Yet courage in pricing is not born of bravado; it is grounded in evidence, discipline, and structure.

The task is to shift from reactive to proactive, from being a price-taker to a price-setter. That requires reframing four areas where businesses commonly falter. First, *anchoring to value rather than fear*—recognising that customers respond less to your costs and more to the value you create, and that framing, tiers, and minimums are tools to shape willingness to pay. Second, recognising that *terms often matter more than tags*: deposits, retainers, and milestone payments protect your capacity and reduce cash risk more effectively than chasing the last pound on sticker price. Third, treating *discounts not as favours but as tools with rules*, setting fences and expirations that preserve contribution margin instead of casually eroding it. Finally, weaving in *indexation and escalators*, mechanisms that ensure long-term contracts remain profitable when costs rise.

The implications are both practical and philosophical. Practically, this means designing structures that change outcomes—contracts that protect production, pricing that anticipates inflation, offers that channel behaviour. Philosophically, it means confronting the psychology of pricing: the tendency to undercharge as an act of insecurity, or to over-discount as a substitute for sales courage. Every misplaced pound tells a story of fear masquerading as strategy.

Pricing, then, is not a static number. It is a living negotiation between value, trust, and survival. The question is whether you will set that negotiation on your own terms, or whether you will let it be dictated by the fears of competitors and the bargaining instincts of customers. The tools in this chapter are not theoretical constructs; they are shields and levers. Used well, they can transform pricing from a source of anxiety into a source of strength.

What happens when you stop treating price as an afterthought and start treating it as the pulse of your business? When you anchor to value, structure your terms, enforce discount discipline, and embed escalators, you move from vanity to viability. But the real challenge lies not in knowing these principles—it lies in applying them when a customer hesitates, a competitor undercuts, or a market shocks. The coming pages will not only map the tools but test your resolve. The silence around pricing ends here. Will you find your voice?

Anchor to value, not to fear

The most common pricing error is not greed but timidity. Walk into any marketplace, from a farmer's stall to a consulting boardroom, and you will often find sellers whispering their own prices as though half-expecting rejection. They glance sideways at competitors, trim a little off their numbers, and hope that volume will compensate for margin. This is not strategy—it is fear disguised as caution. Yet history consistently shows that businesses built on fear rarely endure, while those that anchor their prices to value, rather than to nerves, carve out resilience and authority.

Consider the story of the Montblanc pen. Functionally, it performs the same task as any cheap biro: it transfers ink to paper. Yet Montblanc does not anchor its price to ink or plastic. It anchors to the intangible value of craftsmanship, heritage, and status. Buyers are not calculating cost per written word; they are buying a symbol of permanence and prestige. The pen's value, not its production cost, sets the price. Montblanc could have priced timidly and fought in the trenches of stationery retail. Instead, it had the courage to let value—rather than fear—be the anchor.

The psychology underpinning this is well-studied. Behavioural economists have shown that buyers respond less to absolute prices than to frames and reference points. Present three tiers—basic, standard, premium—and most customers will gravitate to the middle, not because it is objectively best, but because the framing makes it appear safe. Introduce a minimum viable price, and customers interpret it as a marker of quality. Apple does this with ruthless simplicity. Its entry-level products are not designed to be cheap; they are designed to make the mid-tier look irresistible. Anchoring works not by tricking the customer but by clarifying relative value.

For small businesses, this principle is liberating. You do not need the scale of Apple to use framing. A café might offer three coffee sizes, not to sell the smallest, but to steer buyers towards the profitable middle. A freelance designer might package services into clear tiers: a baseline option that feels too thin, a deluxe one that feels indulgent, and a middle tier that feels like common sense. These are not manipulations; they are ways of guiding behaviour while protecting margins. Buyers often want to be steered—they want assurance that they are choosing wisely. Pricing architecture provides that assurance.

The difficulty is not in designing tiers or minimums, but in summoning the courage to implement them. Too many founders anchor to fear: "If I charge more, customers will leave." This objection collapses under scrutiny. Raise your price by 10%. If half your customers fled—a catastrophic scenario—your revenue would be unchanged, while your workload would halve. In practice, far fewer leave, and those who stay signal loyalty and value perception. The result is higher contribution margin and better customers. Fear imagines a mass exodus; evidence shows selective refinement.

Examples abound. Netflix's subscription increases have rarely dented subscriber numbers in proportion to the price change; instead, they have reinforced the perception of premium content. Professional services firms routinely use minimum fees not as exclusionary barriers but as declarations of seriousness. In both cases, the message is the same: price is not just a number; it is a signal of worth. Underpricing does not inspire gratitude; it invites suspicion.

Philosophically, anchoring to value requires a shift in self-perception. If you see your product as a commodity, you will price defensively. If you see it as a solution to a real problem, you will price with confidence. Fear belongs to the mindset of scarcity—assuming the buyer has all the power and you must capitulate. Value belongs to the mindset of agency—recognising that price communicates belief in your own offering. The buyer senses the difference. A fearful seller invites haggling; a value-anchored seller invites trust.

This is not to romanticise price increases. Courage in pricing is not recklessness. It is evidence-based discipline. Anchoring to value means mapping carefully what customers truly care about, where your differentiation lies, and how willingness to pay aligns with outcomes. It is as much data as it is psychology. A SaaS company that ties pricing to saved labour hours or revenue lift is not gambling; it is aligning its fees to measurable impact. A restaurant that prices a set menu higher not because of ingredients alone but because of the crafted experience is monetising its unique value. Courage here is not bluster—it is clarity.

Fear will whisper that competitors are cheaper, that customers are fickle, that a higher number will push them away. Evidence replies with firmness: businesses that price confidently, frame intelligently, and back it with consistent delivery outperform those that race to the bottom. The margin gap is not vanity—it is survival. And survival is not won by those who whisper their worth. It is won by those who state it plainly, anchor it to value, and stand their ground.

The question, then, is simple but sharp: will you let fear set your price, or will you anchor to the value you actually create? Your decision will not only shape your margins—it will shape the kind of business you build, and the kind of customers you attract.

Terms beat tags

In 2008, a boutique architecture firm in London landed what should have been its breakthrough commission: the redesign of a landmark commercial space. The fee, by industry standards, was fair. The team celebrated, mapped out the work, and hired extra hands. But the contract carried a flaw hidden in plain sight. Payment was due only upon completion. Six months later, the firm delivered world-class drawings, received glowing feedback—and waited another four months for payment as the client dragged its heels through "internal processes." By then, the firm's cash reserves had evaporated, the new hires were gone, and the partners had mortgaged their own homes to keep the lights on. Ironically, the list price that looked so good on paper mattered less than the terms that never protected them.

This story is not unusual. Across industries, companies haemorrhage not because they fail to sell, but because they fail to structure how and when they are paid. The paradox is stark: a business can win contracts, boast strong order books, and even post accounting profits, yet collapse in practice because cash comes too late. Entrepreneurs obsess over the price tag, yet the terms attached to that tag are what truly decide whether revenue turns into survival. Terms beat tags because cash flow, not quoted value, is the bloodstream of a business.

The logic is simple yet under-appreciated. A £50,000 project with 30% upfront is radically safer than a £60,000 project paid in arrears. A software subscription billed annually in advance is more powerful than one billed monthly, even at a slightly lower rate. Payment structure is not an afterthought—it is a strategic lever that determines working capital, protects production capacity, and transforms fragile projections into stable reality. Yet many owners negotiate terms timidly, fearing that clients will walk away. In truth, terms rarely kill a deal; more often, they clarify seriousness and professionalism.

Consider the practice of deposits. A deposit does not simply accelerate cash; it creates mutual commitment. When a client places money upfront, they demonstrate belief in the relationship. The provider, in turn, secures the liquidity to allocate resources properly. This symmetry reduces the risk of scope creep and last-minute cancellations. Hotels have long understood this: prepayment locks in revenue and deters frivolous booking. For professional services, deposits function in exactly the same way—protecting time, capacity, and cash.

Milestones extend the logic. Breaking a large project into staged payments not only aligns income with work delivered but disciplines both parties. The client must stay engaged, providing feedback and approvals, while the supplier avoids the temptation to sprint recklessly towards the finish. A digital agency that bills 20% at kick-off, 40% at design sign-off, and 40% on delivery is not being bureaucratic; it is engineering cash cycles that mirror effort. In doing so, it prevents the lopsided risk where months of labour are underwritten by hope rather than bank deposits.

Retainers push the idea further still, transforming lumpy project work into recurring revenue. For a lawyer, a consultant, or a maintenance provider, the retainer ensures that time and expertise are not left vulnerable to erratic demand. Retainers convert uncertainty into predictability. They may require price concessions, but they repay the business in liquidity and stability. To the client, they offer guaranteed access; to the provider, they provide breathing space for investment and planning. Retainers, in effect, replace feast-and-famine cycles with steady pulse.

What unites deposits, milestones, and retainers is not just their impact on cash but their ability to protect *capacity*. A workshop filled with unpaid orders is not a triumph—it is a trap. A consultancy juggling clients that delay payments has little room to serve new ones. Production capacity, whether physical or intellectual, is finite. Terms that secure timely inflows allow a business to reserve that capacity for clients who value it. Those who resist fair terms reveal themselves: they are not serious partners but hidden risks.

There is also a deeper philosophical insight here. Negotiating terms is not about squeezing the other party; it is about designing relationships that are sustainable. A contract that leaves one side gasping for liquidity is not a partnership; it is exploitation by delay. When both sides know that value and cash move together, trust deepens. Far from losing sales, businesses that insist on healthy terms often find they gain respect. Serious clients expect professionals to value their own work. Only the unserious push for credit disguised as convenience.

Evidence shows that terms change outcomes more than tags. Many a company has collapsed chasing "big wins" at prestigious prices, only to discover those prices were payable 120 days after delivery. Meanwhile, leaner rivals thrive by collecting smaller invoices swiftly. Supermarkets demand long credit lines from suppliers; yet those suppliers that survive are those who negotiate shelf fees, promotional contributions, or pre-orders that protect their cash cycles. Price is visible. Terms are structural. The latter determine endurance.

In practice, courage in negotiating terms comes from framing. Rather than apologetically requesting a deposit, present it as a standard: "To reserve production capacity, we require 30% upfront." Rather than pleading for staged payments, frame them as mutual safeguards: "This structure ensures progress is measured and cash flow is fair." Rather than fearing rejection, treat refusal as a signal of risk. If a client cannot afford to share risk upfront, should you afford to shoulder theirs entirely?

The question is not whether terms matter—they always do—but whether leaders will prioritise them as fiercely as they prioritise price. Cash is oxygen. Payment structures determine who breathes easily and who suffocates slowly. The architect who mortgages his home while waiting for a £200,000 cheque is no better off than the freelancer who insists on £5,000 upfront and collects the rest steadily. Both sell services. Only one designs terms.

The unresolved challenge lingers: how much courage are you willing to summon to let terms, not tags, dictate your deals? In that choice lies the difference between revenue that flatters and cash that sustains.

Discounts with rules

In 2019, a fast-growing e-commerce start-up discovered that its most loyal customers were not the ones it thought. They weren't repeat buyers charmed by quality or service. They were professional resellers who had learned how to game the system. By waiting for predictable "holiday sales," stacking promo codes, and exploiting referral schemes, these buyers secured products below cost. The company, eager to show growth, trumpeted record order numbers. But when the dust settled, margins had collapsed, inventory had been distorted, and genuine customers had quietly drifted away. The obsession with discounting—without discipline—had undermined the very unit economics on which survival depended.

The paradox is stark: discounts, intended as a weapon for growth, can become the architect of destruction. When wielded without rules, they do not signal generosity but weakness. When designed carefully, however, discounts can create urgency, reward desired behaviour, and tip the undecided buyer into action—without eroding the financial spine of the business. The difference lies not in whether to discount, but in *how* and *when*.

Every successful enterprise recognises that discounting must be fenced. A fence is a boundary that decides who qualifies, under what conditions, and for how long. Airlines mastered this decades ago: students, early bookers, and off-peak travellers see lower fares, while business travellers pay premium rates. These fences are not arbitrary—they segment buyers by willingness to pay, preserving revenue from those who value flexibility while still filling planes. The same logic applies across industries. A discount without a fence is an open invitation to value destruction. With fences, it becomes a tool of segmentation, separating customers you want from those you cannot afford to subsidise.

Time is the second discipline. Expirations transform a discount from an open wound into a call to action. Without deadlines, buyers delay indefinitely, waiting for better deals. With deadlines, hesitation carries a cost. This is not trickery; it is behavioural economics at work. Human beings respond to scarcity and urgency. A retailer who offers "20% off for the next three days" converts fence-sitters who might otherwise procrastinate. A professional services firm that ties a reduced rate to contracts signed before quarter-end aligns its pipeline with operational planning. Expiration protects both psychology and cash flow.

But fences and expirations are not enough on their own. The financial discipline comes from contribution analysis. Too many teams measure discounts against revenue rather than contribution. A £1,000 sale at 20% off may still sound like income, but if the variable costs are £700, the margin has collapsed from £300 to £100—a two-thirds drop in profit. The rule of thumb is simple: unless a discount preserves contribution, it risks destroying more value than it creates. This logic forces leaders to ask: *Does this discount drive incremental volume that more than covers the lost margin?* If not, it is a vanity move, not a strategy.

Disciplined companies train their teams to see this distinction. A salesperson under pressure to close a deal will always find it tempting to give away 10% "just this once." Left unchecked, this behaviour normalises. Suddenly, the market expects discounts as standard, and list prices become ornamental. By embedding rules—such as requiring managerial approval for discounts above a certain threshold, or limiting discounts to specific customer categories—leaders ensure that generosity does not metastasise into habit. The discipline lies not in saying *never,* but in saying *only if.*

The psychology of framing matters, too. A discount presented as a reward feels different from one presented as a concession. Offering "preferred pricing for early partners" signals inclusion and exclusivity. Offering "10% off because you asked" signals desperation. The same percentage can carry radically different meanings depending on the story attached. Businesses that frame discounts as part of a deliberate structure reinforce their brand; those that use them as panic buttons dilute it.

Examples abound. Supermarkets use loyalty cards not just to offer discounts but to tie them to data collection, shaping future behaviour. SaaS companies offer annual billing discounts not as random generosity but as a lever to secure upfront cash and reduce churn. Fitness gyms fence discounts by offering off-peak memberships for students, while protecting prime-time pricing for professionals. Each case shows that discounts, when fenced and timed, can support strategy. When sprayed indiscriminately, they corrode it.

The deeper insight is this: discounting is not merely about numbers; it is about culture. An organisation that allows its sales team to slash prices unchecked has surrendered its sense of value. One that insists on rules signals internally and externally that value is non-negotiable. Customers sense this discipline. Investors reward it. Staff respect it. The cost of undisciplined discounting is not just margin erosion—it is institutional fragility.

And so the unresolved tension remains: can your business create a system where discounts serve as precise instruments, not blunt weapons? Can you design fences and expirations that protect contribution without stifling growth? Or will you, like so many firms before, discover too late that in chasing revenue through indiscriminate generosity, you have quietly dismantled the very foundations of profit?

Indexation and escalators

In the 1970s, when oil prices quadrupled almost overnight, companies locked into long-term supply contracts without price-adjustment clauses watched their margins evaporate. What had looked like reliable, predictable revenue streams turned into slow-motion losses, draining cash and morale in equal measure. By contrast, firms that had tied their contracts to oil indices or inflation benchmarks weathered the storm with relative stability. The lesson was brutal but clear: value that is not protected in writing will be surrendered in practice.

The paradox of long-term agreements is that they offer security at the cost of flexibility. A five-year contract gives both parties confidence to plan ahead, but over such a span, input costs can shift dramatically—labour, raw materials, shipping, energy, even compliance fees. Without a mechanism for adjustment, what begins as a fair exchange can curdle into exploitation, often unintentionally. A supplier struggling under rising costs may resent the customer who insists on fixed terms. A customer blindsided by sudden surcharges may feel betrayed. Indexation and escalator clauses exist to prevent this erosion of trust. They are not instruments of greed but of continuity.

Indexation works by tethering contract prices to an external measure—a published index of commodity prices, consumer inflation, or sector-specific inputs. Escalators, in turn, specify the cadence and formula of adjustment. A construction firm, for example, may include a clause tying steel and cement costs to government-published materials indices, with semi-annual recalculations. A software vendor might link support fees to a wage index, recognising that salaries, not servers, drive its long-term costs. The detail varies, but the principle remains: the contract moves with the world rather than against it.

Critics sometimes object that indexation feels confrontational, as if signalling distrust in the other party's fairness. Yet the opposite is true. By externalising adjustments to neutral data, the negotiation becomes less personal and more objective. Instead of haggling each year over why a service "must" cost more, both sides agree to a formula in advance. The discussion shifts from subjective persuasion to shared reference points. In practice, this often strengthens relationships, because the contract is seen as both resilient and fair.

The art, of course, lies in implementation. Client-friendly language is essential. Saying "fees will rise annually by CPI" is blunt; saying "to ensure service continuity and invest in the staff and systems that support you, fees will adjust modestly in line with published inflation figures" is persuasive. Both sentences deliver the same mechanics, but one frames the adjustment as protection of partnership rather than extraction. The same principle applies to timing: automatic annual reviews feel routine, whereas ad hoc increases feel opportunistic. Predictability breeds acceptance.

Escalators are not just defensive tools. They can actively shape competitive strategy. A company that standardises them across contracts can confidently bid for larger projects, knowing it will not be trapped in future losses. It can also manage investor expectations with greater precision: a revenue stream indexed to inflation carries less uncertainty than one subject to arbitrary renegotiations. In industries where margins are thin, the difference between with and without escalators is not theoretical—it is existential.

Consider a professional services firm. Its greatest cost is talent. If salaries rise by 5% a year but client contracts remain fixed, the firm's margin will collapse within three years. Adding a wage-linked escalator ensures continuity. For subscription-based technology platforms, the risk may be cloud hosting or cybersecurity compliance fees. An index tied to those inputs ensures that the customer shares the burden of systemic shifts rather than leaving the provider to absorb them. Each business must identify its most volatile input and craft its escalator around that risk.

There are, of course, tensions. Customers often push back, fearing they will lose control of costs. Here again, transparency is the antidote. Explaining the rationale—*this clause ensures service quality without sudden shocks*—helps align interests. Some firms even cap escalators, offering predictability while still protecting a baseline of viability. Others offer customers the option of fixed terms at a premium, effectively charging for certainty. In either case, the key is choice: escalation feels punitive only when imposed without explanation or alternatives.

The absence of escalators is itself a gamble, one that rarely pays off. History shows that shocks—whether oil embargoes, financial crises, or pandemic disruptions—arrive more frequently than executives like to admit. Each shock exposes the fragility of contracts that assumed stability. By contrast, organisations that embed indexation clauses into their standard playbook are less exposed. They may still feel the tremors, but they will not be shattered by them.

The unresolved question, then, is cultural as much as contractual: will your business treat indexation as an awkward afterthought, raised reluctantly at the end of negotiation, or as a standard practice woven into every agreement? If the latter, you protect not only your margins but also the long-term trust of your clients. If the former, you risk selling predictability today at the expense of survival tomorrow. Which choice better reflects the business you aspire to build?

Chapter 5
Break-Even and the Shape of Risk

In 1972, a small family-owned airline in the United States discovered, almost by accident, the precise number of tickets it had to sell on each flight to avoid financial collapse. It wasn't a round figure or a comfortable average—it was a line drawn with brutal clarity between solvency and failure. Sell fewer than sixty-two seats, and the airline bled money. Sell sixty-three, and it lived to fly another day. What astonished its founders was not just the number itself, but how invisible it had been until the crisis forced them to calculate it. The break-even point was not a detail of accounting—it was the business itself laid bare.

Every enterprise, whether a corner café, a software start-up, or a multinational manufacturer, lives in the shadow of its break-even line. Yet many leaders talk about growth, innovation, and expansion without truly knowing where survival begins. Numbers are tossed about—runway, margins, burn rate—but too often they obscure more than they reveal. The paradox is that businesses spend energy forecasting distant futures while ignoring the point where tomorrow may not come at all. Break-even is not a mathematical curiosity; it is the most honest mirror a business can face.

To map that mirror requires stripping away illusions. Founders often exclude their own salaries when drawing up fixed costs, as if their time is somehow free. Leases are treated as background noise rather than non-negotiable obligations. "Optional" costs are presented as discretionary long after they have ossified into recurring commitments. The result is a misleading portrait of resilience. Only when every cost—payroll, rent, software licences, and the founder's own labour—is placed on the table does the runway appear for what it is: finite, inflexible, and demanding of hard choices.

But the break-even question grows more complex as products diversify. A microbrewery selling pints at its bar, kegs to restaurants, and branded merchandise online cannot rely on a single break-even figure. Each revenue stream has its own margin and demand cycle, and collapsing them into one number risks distortion. Here, a weighted method is essential—a basket view that reflects both the mix of sales and the contribution each brings. For the brewery, this might mean calculating how many kegs offset the fixed costs of brewing, how many pints smooth the cash flow, and how many T-shirts are needed to make the expansion worthwhile. What emerges is not a neat point but a usable band—a shaded zone within which survival, risk, and opportunity intersect.

Operating near that zone exposes both peril and potential. A small swing in demand or pricing can turn losses into profits—or the reverse. This is operational leverage: the multiplier effect of fixed costs. For the well-prepared, leverage is a tool, enabling a modest increase in sales to produce dramatic gains. For the unprepared, it is a trap, magnifying volatility until it overwhelms cash reserves. The art of management is to understand this leverage in advance, to quantify the upside and downside, and to set guardrails that prevent euphoria from outpacing prudence. Hiring decisions, marketing spend, and expansion bets should all be tested against this dynamic—not in theory, but in real numbers that show what a change of 5 per cent in volume or price means for the bank account.

Yet even with maps and guardrails, no business can predict the future perfectly. This is why the most resilient leaders build what might be called a shut-off plan. They decide in advance under what conditions they will pause a campaign, close a product line, or pivot to a new model. Crucially, these decisions are documented—not left to be argued in the fog of crisis when emotions cloud judgement. A well-crafted shut-off plan turns the abstract shape of risk into an actionable playbook. It ensures that when the time comes, choices are made with discipline rather than desperation.

The shape of risk, then, is not a shadow to fear but a contour to study. Break-even is not merely a threshold but a landscape—fixed costs carving the terrain, product mix altering its slope, operational leverage sharpening its cliffs, and shut-off rules providing the escape routes. To understand this shape is to move from drifting at the mercy of events to navigating with intent.

The question that lingers is deceptively simple: will you confront your break-even line when it is still a tool for decision, or only when it becomes a verdict handed down by your bank balance? The answer will define not just the lifespan of your business, but the kind of risks you take, the kind of resilience you build, and ultimately the kind of leader you become.

The honest fixed-cost map

In 2008, as the financial crisis rippled across the globe, countless entrepreneurs discovered a brutal truth: the optionality they thought they had in their budgets did not exist. Marketing "cuts" that were pencilled in as levers of survival could not be executed without choking demand. Founders who had treated their own salaries as flexible suddenly found themselves unable to pay rent or groceries. What brought them down was not the collapse of demand alone but a profound miscalculation of their *true* fixed costs. They had mistaken hope for optionality, and the market exposed the illusion.

The paradox of fixed costs is that they are both obvious and invisible. Obvious because they sit, month after month, on invoices and payroll schedules. Invisible because entrepreneurs convince themselves they can defer or renegotiate them when the moment comes. The lease is "flexible" because a landlord *might* agree to terms. The founder's pay is "discretionary" because passion will carry the day. Software subscriptions are "optional" because they can be cancelled with a few clicks. Yet when pressure arrives, almost none of these costs actually move. To misclassify them is not a harmless oversight but a distortion of reality, one that inflates resilience and shrinks perceived risk.

An honest fixed-cost map begins with the refusal to flinch. It requires laying out, line by line, every obligation that cannot be shed without damaging the very ability to trade. Founder pay belongs here, not in some parallel column of deferred dreams. If the business does not generate enough to cover the founder's livelihood, then what is being measured is not viability but subsidy. Similarly, leases and long-term commitments must be acknowledged for what they are: unyielding anchors. By assembling these into a fixed-cost table, the entrepreneur moves from wishful abstraction to a ledger of reality.

When that table is complete, it does more than produce a monthly number; it reveals a runway. The cash balance divided by fixed burn is not just arithmetic—it is time itself quantified. And time, unlike money, cannot be borrowed back. A company that has six months of fixed-cost coverage is not "nimble" or "flexible." It has exactly six months to reach breakeven or secure new funding. Pretending otherwise is a luxury the bank balance does not permit.

The discipline of mapping fixed costs extends beyond survival. It shapes strategic clarity. Consider two cafés on opposite sides of a city. One rents a small unit with modest seating; the other has signed a ten-year lease in a high-footfall location. Their variable costs—beans, milk, staff hours—are similar, but their fixed-cost structures create entirely different strategic postures. The first can experiment, close on quiet days, or pivot to takeaway models. The second must drive relentless volume to justify its rent. The honest map shows not only the *what* of survival but the *how* of strategy.

Technology businesses face a different but no less binding trap. Founders often understate fixed commitments to software infrastructure, cloud services, or developer salaries by imagining that "scalability" will soften the burden. In practice, these costs harden quickly into the base load of operations. What appears flexible at the seed stage becomes immovable by the time customers depend on uptime. Here again, an honest fixed-cost map unmasks the reality: optionality is not optional when the alternative is reputational ruin.

The intellectual challenge is not in compiling the numbers but in accepting their authority. Human beings are wired for optimism; entrepreneurs even more so. Optimism treats fixed costs as negotiable, as if the world will yield under the pressure of conviction. Reality says otherwise. To decide with the real number is to accept a kind of humility—an admission that the business must work within limits that no amount of passion or ingenuity can erase.

And yet, within those limits lies liberation. A founder who knows the true fixed burn is free to plan honestly, to design campaigns that respect the runway, to negotiate from a place of clarity. Investors respond differently to leaders who present a fixed-cost table that includes their own pay—because it signals both professionalism and self-respect.

Staff take confidence from leaders who do not spin tales of optionality but confront constraints openly. The fixed-cost map, far from being a cage, becomes a compass.

The lingering question is not whether a business can assemble its fixed costs—it can—but whether its leaders are willing to look unflinchingly at the number that results. Can they resist the seduction of imagined flexibility? Can they accept that the most important decision they will make is not about scaling, fundraising, or product features, but about how many months of survival they truly command? Until that question is answered with rigour, every other decision floats in air. Only when the honest map is drawn does the ground beneath the business finally come into view.

Multi-product break-even

Every small business owner longs for a single number—a line on the wall or in a spreadsheet—that says, "This is the point at which you break even." It is comforting, definitive, and, in most cases, a fiction. For the café that sells both cappuccinos and sandwiches, for the consultancy that blends fixed retainers with ad hoc projects, for the brewery that pours pints while wholesaling bottles, there is no single number. There is a shifting landscape of mixes, margins, and weightings. To cling to one neat figure is to court miscalculation.

The paradox is obvious in practice but routinely ignored in planning. If a business sells three products with radically different margins, break-even cannot be expressed as one crisp threshold. Sell more of the high-margin line and break-even is reached earlier; push too much volume of the low-margin product and it recedes further away. The neat, singular break-even figure in many business plans is less a forecast than a guess. Yet the discipline of weighted analysis provides a path to rigour, one that transforms intuition into clarity.

Consider the case of a micro-brewery. The founders brew three varieties: a premium craft IPA sold directly in the taproom, a mid-range lager sold in bottles to local shops, and kegs of a session ale distributed to pubs. Each carries a different price point and, more importantly, a different margin structure. The taproom pint, though sold at a lower volume, yields a generous contribution after costs. The bottled lager produces slimmer margins but has steady demand. The kegs move in bulk but command the lowest margin, especially after delivery costs.

Now imagine the brewery's accountant announcing that the business needs to sell 5,000 units a month to break even. The statement sounds authoritative—yet what does it mean? Five thousand pints in the taproom? Impossible, given capacity. Five thousand kegs? Catastrophic, given the margin. The reality is that the mix matters as much as the total. To build a meaningful break-even, the brewery must weight each product line by its contribution margin and its likely share of sales. Only then can the threshold be represented with accuracy.

The weighted method begins with contribution margins per unit: how much each product adds to covering fixed costs once variable costs are stripped out. Next comes the sales mix—what proportion of each product the business expects to sell. Multiply and combine, and the result is not a number but a *band*. A range within which the business will break even, depending on shifts in mix. For the brewery, the band might show that with a steady flow of taproom sales, break-even arrives at 3,000–3,500 units. Without them, even 6,000 units might fail to cover costs.

This band is not a weakness but a strength. It reflects reality: businesses rarely hit precise forecasts but often fluctuate within ranges. A break-even band sets guardrails, allowing leaders to see where risk lies. It also focuses attention on the products that matter most. In the brewery example, management can see that protecting taproom traffic is disproportionately important. Losing a handful of high-margin pints cannot be offset by thousands of low-margin kegs. The numbers force the realisation: not all sales are created equal.

The philosophical lesson is sobering. We crave certainty, a single beacon in the fog of commerce. Weighted break-even denies us that comfort. It demands acceptance of complexity, and with it, discipline. Leaders who grasp this are less likely to be blindsided. They stop celebrating "record sales months" without asking *which* products drove them. They stop assuming growth solves everything. They start managing mix as carefully as volume.

Weighted break-even also changes behaviour under stress. When sales dip, the instinct is often to push volume wherever possible. But if that push accelerates low-margin products, the business can grow itself into deeper losses. A weighted analysis reveals this trap in advance, showing which lines can safely absorb pressure and which turn additional sales into quicksand.

The broader insight reaches beyond breweries and cafés. In any organisation with multiple revenue streams—software firms with tiered subscriptions, consultancies with retainer and project work, manufacturers with premium and budget ranges—the weighted method exposes hidden vulnerabilities. It gives language to an essential reality: risk is not evenly spread. Every business carries products that pull disproportionate weight.

The danger of one-number thinking is not only miscalculation but complacency. It allows leaders to tell themselves they are "on track" while drifting into fragility. A weighted break-even band, by contrast, is a living map of survival. It acknowledges uncertainty but offers structure. It forces honesty about which parts of the business are indispensable and which are ballast.

And yet, it leaves one question unresolved: what happens when the mix itself shifts in ways no spreadsheet foresaw? What if the high-margin line falters, not from neglect but from changing taste, regulation, or competition? The band gives clarity but not immunity. It sharpens the view but does not guarantee the ground beneath will hold. That tension—the interplay between analysis and unpredictability—defines the true challenge of break-even in a multi-product world. To grasp it is to step closer to mastery; to ignore it is to live with illusions that no number, however neat, can defend.

Operational leverage

There is a peculiar cruelty to operational leverage: it flatters in good times and punishes in bad, and it does so with disproportionate force. A company hovering near break-even discovers this truth the hard way. A modest uptick in revenue suddenly propels profit margins skyward, making the business appear like a finely tuned machine. Yet the same mechanics work in reverse: a small stumble in sales can unravel cash reserves at alarming speed. The same structure that fuels the dream of scalability also amplifies fragility.

Think of an airline. The majority of its costs—aircraft leases, salaries, maintenance—are fixed, paid whether planes fly full or half empty. Each additional ticket sold above break-even is almost pure contribution to profit, making the industry intoxicating when demand is strong. But when seats go unsold, those same fixed costs turn into anchors. The line between success and collapse can be just a few percentage points of load factor. That knife-edge, familiar to airlines, is replicated in countless smaller businesses with high fixed cost bases: gyms, co-working spaces, SaaS platforms, manufacturers with expensive equipment. The mathematics of leverage is universal, even if its expression varies.

At the core of operational leverage lies a simple ratio: how much of your cost base is fixed relative to variable. A company with heavy fixed commitments—rent, salaries, long-term contracts—will see profits accelerate more dramatically once revenue exceeds break-even, because each incremental sale carries little additional cost. Conversely, before break-even, every missed unit widens the gap at the same dramatic pace. Businesses with mostly variable costs—say, a freelance agency that scales contractors per project—lack this upside, but they also avoid the violent downside. Leverage is neither inherently good nor bad; it is exposure, a multiplier of both fortune and error.

To manage that exposure, leaders must first *quantify* it. That means modelling not just average outcomes but sensitivities around them: what happens if revenue dips by 5 per cent? What if demand spikes by 10? The volatility around break-even is rarely linear. A 5 per cent swing in revenue can lead to a 50 per cent swing in profit or loss, depending on structure. Mapping this range forces a more sober conversation about risk appetite. Do you have the cash runway to survive the downside? Are you prepared for the hiring demands of the upside?

Consider a software firm with £2 million in fixed annual costs—developers, licences, office overhead. Its variable cost per customer is negligible. At £2 million in revenue, the company is break-even. At £2.1 million, it suddenly records £100,000 profit—a 5 per cent revenue increase produces infinite margin expansion from zero. But reverse the scenario: £1.9 million revenue now creates a £100,000 loss. In both directions, leverage magnifies small changes into existential outcomes.

The practical response is to establish *guardrails*. Spending and hiring cannot simply follow optimism. They must be tethered to thresholds that reflect the volatility of the model. Leaders might commit to new hires only once revenue sustains 120 per cent of break-even for three consecutive quarters, or they might cap marketing spend to ensure cash buffers cover at least six months of downside risk. Guardrails make leverage intentional rather than accidental.

But operational leverage is not only about financial ratios; it is about psychology. When growth accelerates, the temptation is to extrapolate straight lines into the future and commit to expansion—larger offices, bigger payrolls, new product lines. Leaders talk themselves into permanence on the back of temporary surges. This is where volatility becomes lethal: optimism hardens into fixed commitments just as conditions change. Wise managers resist by treating each expansion decision as a bet with known odds, asking not just *what is the upside?* but *what is the cash cost of being wrong?*

The inverse psychological trap appears in downturns. Faced with losses magnified by leverage, leaders can overcorrect, slashing too deeply and damaging long-term capacity. Here, too, discipline is essential. Pre-drafted contingency plans—rules about when to cut, pause, or pivot—stop panic from dictating strategy. They anchor decisions in prior clarity rather than present fear.

Operational leverage also shapes competitive dynamics. A business with high fixed costs can be more aggressive in markets where utilisation is everything, knowing that once capacity is covered, additional volume is disproportionately valuable. This explains why gyms push aggressively for new members even when facilities look full, or why airlines compete fiercely for marginal routes. They are chasing contribution above the line, because below it lies ruin. For low-leverage businesses, competition plays differently: survival comes not from volume but from margin discipline.

What emerges is a richer understanding of leverage not as a static condition but as a living risk profile. It demands continuous reassessment, because the balance of fixed and variable costs shifts with each contract signed, each hire made, each lease renewed. Leaders who fail to revisit their leverage model are often surprised by volatility they themselves engineered.

Yet even with guardrails, forecasts, and contingency plans, one uncomfortable truth remains: leverage makes you faster, but it also makes you less stable. It sharpens both opportunity and risk. The question is not whether to embrace it—most businesses cannot avoid it entirely—but how consciously you carry it.

So the real challenge is not to calculate operational leverage once, but to live with it daily: to let it inform hiring, pricing, expansion, and restraint. The reward is clarity in moments when optimism or fear might otherwise overwhelm judgement. The penalty for neglect is to wake up one morning and realise that the shape of your risk, long ignored, has already struck the balance sheet.

And still, the question lingers: if leverage is both your accelerant and your hazard, how much of it should you dare to hold?

The shut-off plan

There is a strange irony at the heart of business failure: most companies do not die because they never had a chance; they die because they waited too long to stop. Leaders cling to projects, campaigns, and product lines with the hope that another week, another client, another tweak will tip the balance. Yet the bank account is indifferent to optimism. It counts only pounds and pence. By the time reality forces a decision, the choice is no longer about strategy—it is about survival, and options have vanished.

History is littered with examples. Consider Kodak, a company that invented digital photography but clung to film for too long, bleeding cash while pretending it could sustain both. Or the countless start-ups that launch a promising product, see weak traction, and then burn millions in a desperate attempt to "buy time," only to find themselves out of runway. The brutal truth is that a shut-off plan, made in advance, could have saved many of them—not necessarily the product, but the company itself. The failure was not that they experimented, but that they lacked the discipline to pre-commit to *when to stop*.

The essence of a shut-off plan is pre-decision. It is not an improvisation under duress but a deliberate commitment made when heads are cool, cash is stable, and perspective is intact. It forces leaders to ask: under what conditions will we pause this campaign? When will we discontinue this product line? What signals will trigger a pivot? Without those thresholds, every debate in the heat of crisis becomes a fog of sunk costs and personal pride.

A proper plan begins with documented *thresholds*. These are not vague notions of "underperformance" but quantifiable measures: cost per acquisition exceeding £200 for three consecutive months; fewer than 100 active users per location after two quarters; churn above 12 per cent despite retention efforts. Numbers turn argument into clarity. They strip the decision of wishful framing and make the rules visible to all stakeholders—founders, managers, investors.

Equally vital are *owners*. Every plan requires a person accountable for pulling the brake. Without explicit responsibility, inertia wins. In many teams, everyone knows something should be stopped, but no one wants to own the act of shutting it down. By naming the decision-maker and backing them with authority, the business ensures that hesitation does not drain precious weeks of cash.

Practising the decision may sound excessive, but it is indispensable. Just as emergency drills prepare crews to act without hesitation, rehearsing the act of shutting off a project makes it less psychologically jarring. A founder who has walked through the steps of pausing a campaign—informing staff, reallocating budget, communicating with investors—will act more decisively when the threshold is crossed. The rehearsal builds not only readiness but resilience.

This discipline also reframes risk. Many leaders think of risk as uncertainty about whether an initiative will succeed. But there is a deeper risk: failing to recognise when it is time to stop. A company that builds its shut-off plan into every new venture transforms uncertainty into bounded exposure. The upside remains intact, but the downside is capped. It is, in effect, an insurance policy paid not with premiums but with foresight.

Consider a small brewery launching a seasonal ale. The temptation is to keep producing as long as there are some sales, even if margins shrink and shelf space tightens. With a shut-off plan, the brewery decides in advance: if weekly sales drop below X cases, we stop production, no matter what. The result is a disciplined allocation of brewing capacity, preserving cash and freeing resources for the next profitable line. The alternative is a slow bleed—warehouses filled with unsold stock and capital locked in sunk inventory.

The challenge, of course, is emotional. Shutting down a project often means admitting error or abandoning a cherished vision. Leaders are not just accountants; they are humans with pride and hope. This is why the shut-off plan must be crafted *before* emotions cloud judgement, and why it should be treated not as a sign of weakness but as evidence of professionalism. Investors, employees, and customers alike respect leaders who know when to pivot with discipline rather than flounder in denial.

Yet there remains an unresolved tension. To innovate, businesses must take risks, and risk-taking inevitably means some experiments fail. How do you preserve courage while embedding discipline? How do you ensure that pre-committed thresholds do not stifle boldness? The answer lies not in avoiding risk, but in building a culture where risk is taken within defined guardrails. Teams can pursue ambitious projects precisely because they know the cost of failure has been pre-limited.

The shut-off plan, then, is not about pessimism. It is about respect—respect for cash, respect for time, respect for the opportunity cost of every decision. It is a reminder that discipline is not the enemy of ambition but its partner. A business that knows when to stop can afford to start more often, to try again, and to survive long enough to find the initiatives that truly scale.

But perhaps the most unsettling question is this: when your next project stumbles—and some inevitably will—will you have the courage to shut it down by design, or will you wait until the bank balance makes the decision for you?

Chapter 6
Build the 13-Week Model

It is a curious truth of business that most companies go bankrupt on a spreadsheet long before they collapse in reality. The warning signs are there—hidden in overdue invoices, in rent commitments, in a payroll date creeping closer than the receivables ledger admits. Yet too often, leaders fly blind, operating with vague projections or the false comfort of annual budgets that bear little resemblance to the rhythm of cash. The crisis comes not as a thunderbolt, but as a slow leak. And when the account finally runs dry, the surprise is not that it happened—it is that it wasn't seen sooner.

The 13-week cash model exists to prevent that blindness. Not as a theoretical exercise in planning, but as a tool designed to match the real cadence of money leaving and entering a bank account. Thirteen weeks is just over three months: long enough to spot danger before it becomes terminal, short enough to grasp without drowning in abstraction. It is the window in which payrolls are met, invoices are chased, suppliers are appeased, and strategy collides with cash reality. This horizon does not ask for perfection; it demands discipline.

For decades, the most resilient operators—turnaround professionals, private equity managers, wartime CFOs—have relied on this tool not because it is sophisticated but because it is brutally honest. It reduces every grand strategy, every visionary promise, every optimistic sales pipeline, to one question: what happens to the bank balance in the next 90 days? In its clarity lies its power.

Building the model is not an accounting ritual but an act of leadership. It forces hard choices about how to structure information, which assumptions to believe, and how to embed the model in weekly discipline. It is not enough to create it once; it must become a living system that drives conversations, decisions, and behaviours. Done well, it becomes the scoreboard that prevents paralysis and replaces fear with foresight.

The chapter begins by showing how to construct the sheet itself: not a labyrinth of tabs and formulas, but a clean line-by-line structure tied directly to bank categories. By mirroring the very statements that govern your liquidity, the model eliminates false comfort and prevents "version chaos." Here, simplicity is strength—a template anyone can edit in one sitting, with names and conventions that mean the same thing to every person who touches it.

From there, the focus shifts to the *collections calendar*. Too many forecasts collapse because they treat due dates as destiny. Clients rarely pay when invoices say they will; they pay when acceptance, approvals, and nudges align. By translating invoices into actual expected receipts—and then embedding weekly calls and scripts—the model replaces wishful thinking with predictable rhythm. Done right, it shrinks days sales outstanding not by magic, but by making collections a managed process rather than an afterthought.

Next comes scenario thinking: the recognition that no single forecast will ever be true. Businesses stumble when they cling to one version of the future, only to be blindsided by the inevitable deviations. A robust 13-week model introduces toggles—base, stretch, and storm cases—with clearly defined triggers. This approach forces leadership teams to decide in advance how they will act under different conditions, rather than improvising under pressure. The ease of switching between scenarios is not a convenience but a survival mechanism.

Finally, reconciliation closes the loop. Every week, forecasted numbers meet actuals. Variance is not a failure but a teacher—if the team is willing to ask why. Did a client delay payment? Did a supplier shift terms? Did internal optimism creep into the assumptions? Capturing these reasons turns misses into sharper models. The point is not blame but learning: each week makes the next week more accurate, until the model becomes a genuine reflection of business reality.

The 13-week model is, at its core, a discipline in truth-telling. It strips away illusions, forces clarity, and replaces vague hope with numbers that demand a response. It is not glamorous, but it is decisive. Leaders who master it can see the shape of risk before it materialises and can navigate volatility without panic. Those who neglect it, by contrast, hand control of their company's fate to chance and timing.

The question is not whether uncertainty will come—it will. The question is whether, when it does, you will already have the sheet in front of you, the thresholds agreed, and the next move clear. Or whether, like so many before, you will look at an empty bank account and wonder how it could have happened so quickly.

Inputs, logic, and structure — Construct the sheet line by line with bank-matched categories. Provide a minimal template and naming convention. Prevent version chaos. Keep it editable in one sitting.

In 2008, a distressed retailer invited in a restructuring firm after months of dwindling cash. The executives, exhausted and anxious, produced spreadsheets that looked impressive—thick with colour-coded tabs, embedded formulas, and financial jargon. Yet when the consultants opened the company's actual bank statements, a simple question brought the room to silence: "Which number on your spreadsheet matches this balance?" Nobody could answer. The survival of the business had been wagered on complexity that no longer tied to reality. Within weeks, the company folded—not because there was no money, but because leaders didn't know how much there really was, or when it would run out.

The lesson endures: a cash forecast is only as strong as the line it can draw back to the bank. A model that dazzles in design but diverges from actual cash flow is worse than useless—it breeds false confidence. By contrast, a sheet that mirrors the bank account in its categories, structure, and naming conventions grounds the business in reality. It trades glamour for clarity, sophistication for survival.

The first principle is to keep the structure minimal. Every extra line is a temptation to over-model; every vague category is a hiding place for assumptions. Begin with the categories your bank recognises: incoming receipts, payroll, rent, utilities, tax, supplier payments. Match them line for line. This mirroring matters not only for reconciliation but also for discipline—when the bank statement arrives, you should be able to check the model without debate over which expense belongs where.

This minimalism also protects against what might be called *version chaos*. Too many businesses fracture their cash forecasts across different files: one spreadsheet for sales, another for overheads, a "master" file with summary numbers. Soon, discrepancies creep in. Which file is the truth? Which tab reflects the latest discussion? When the finance lead is off sick, can anyone else interpret the colour-coded labyrinth? A single editable sheet, built in one sitting, eliminates these fractures. Its authority lies in its simplicity: everyone is looking at the same thing, and what they see is recognisable.

Naming conventions are equally strategic. Labels should be plain, specific, and stable. "Payroll – UK Staff" is better than "People" or "Wages." "Rent – London HQ" is better than "Facilities." Ambiguity kills reconciliation; it allows categories to shift meaning over time. Standardisation prevents that erosion. Even a small team benefits: when one person leaves, another can step in and know immediately what each line means. Precision in naming turns the spreadsheet from a private code into a common language.

Philosophically, this approach recognises a deeper tension: humans crave precision, but precision in finance is often false. You can't know to the penny what will be paid in or out three weeks from now. What you can know is structure. The model isn't about prediction; it is about organisation. By disciplining the inputs and logic, you create a framework that allows uncertainty to surface honestly rather than hide in vague assumptions. The irony is that restraint—keeping the model lean, mirroring the bank, locking the categories—produces more truth than elaborate forecasting ever can.

Consider a minimal template: a weekly grid across the top, cash in and cash out grouped by type down the side. Rows include Receipts, VAT refunds, Payroll, Rent, Utilities, Supplier Payments, Tax. Subtotals show net movement per week, with a running balance reconciled to the opening bank cash. Nothing more. Resist the urge to fragment rent into ten subcategories, or to list every supplier individually. The objective is not accounting detail but operational foresight. You are not building the archive of record—you are building the decision-making dashboard.

A story illustrates the difference. A small design agency once expanded its model into fifty rows of client-specific inflows and vendor-specific outflows. It looked thorough. Yet when one major client delayed payment, the model did not flag the impact until the next reconciliation, because the delay was hidden under "Client B – Phase 3 deliverable" rather than simply "Receipts." The granularity disguised the risk. Only when the model was rebuilt around broad categories did the team see what mattered: the company could not meet payroll in week eleven without collections accelerating. That clarity saved them.

Editing in one sitting is not just a practical suggestion—it is a discipline. A model that sprawls over weeks of tinkering loses coherence. Assumptions harden into errors, categories drift, and formulas are forgotten. By constraining the task to a focused session, you force the design to remain minimal and the naming consistent. The discipline of brevity becomes a safeguard.

There is also a psychological dimension: leaders are more likely to trust and use a tool they understand. A spreadsheet too complex to grasp in an hour will not be sustained. It will be avoided, then abandoned. A sheet that can be taught to a new manager in fifteen minutes becomes part of the weekly cadence. Trust grows not from technical cleverness but from accessibility.

Seen this way, the *inputs, logic, and structure* of a cash model are not trivial housekeeping—they are strategic. They determine whether the business can see itself clearly enough to act. A model that mirrors the bank and enforces discipline in categories allows the organisation to argue about real decisions—pricing, hiring, investment—instead of debating whose spreadsheet is right.

The deeper question is this: do you want a model that impresses, or a model that survives? The ornate construction dazzles in a boardroom but collapses in the field. The plain, disciplined sheet may look unsophisticated, but it delivers the one thing that matters: truth tied to cash. And truth, in finance, is the rarest and most valuable currency of all.

Collections calendar — Translate invoices into expected receipts by acceptance dates. Drive weekly calls and scripts. Replace wishful due dates with reality. Shrink DSO with rhythm.

In a small London consultancy, the founders believed their balance sheet was healthy. Sales were booked, invoices were issued, and the revenue graph glowed upwards. Yet every Friday the same crisis struck: the bank balance sagged lower than expected, payroll loomed, and the partners were forced into emergency calls with clients who had not paid. Contracts said "Net 30," but money rarely arrived in thirty days. Hope had been mistaken for cash. Six months later, despite strong sales, the firm was dismantled. The business had not run out of work—it had run out of rhythm.

The paradox of growth is that companies collapse not for lack of revenue, but for lack of receipts. An invoice is not money. A due date is not a promise. Collections are not an afterthought to sales but their completion, the final transfer from "we have won the work" to "we can fund the next cycle." Yet many organisations treat receivables as if they were fixed, certain, and automatic. They mistake *papered optimism* for liquidity, when in fact, the discipline of collections is the closest thing a business has to a heartbeat.

To bring order to this, leaders must abandon the fiction of invoice due dates as indicators of when cash will actually arrive. Clients pay when they process, not when you bill. Bureaucracy, approval cycles, and human habit insert delays that no contract clause can wish away. The remedy is the *collections calendar*: a tool that maps receivables not to due dates, but to *acceptance dates*—the point at which the client has truly acknowledged and queued the payment. This calendar translates "what we are owed" into "what we can expect." It replaces spreadsheets full of wishful arithmetic with something more grounded: a rhythm of receipts.

The difference is more than semantic. A due date is static; it tells you nothing about behaviour. An acceptance date, by contrast, is dynamic. It acknowledges that cash comes when procurement clears the invoice, when finance runs the batch, when a manager approves the milestone. A collections calendar, line by line, forces the business to trace when each invoice is likely to convert. By doing so, it turns receivables into a forecast rather than a hope.

Consider how powerful this becomes when tied to weekly cadence. A company that schedules collections calls every Thursday, aligned with the calendar, shifts from reactive chasing to proactive rhythm. Staff know which invoices are due for confirmation, which need escalation, which can be nudged with a polite script. Clients, too, adjust: the vendor who calls consistently, professionally, and on time gets paid sooner than the one who sends sporadic reminders. Over weeks, days sales outstanding (DSO) compresses, not by luck but by discipline.

Scripts matter here. Too many finance teams call debtors with vague phrases—"Just checking on the invoice"—that give clients room to deflect. A disciplined script ties the call to a specific acceptance step: "We see the invoice entered on 14 June. Can you confirm it is scheduled for the 30 June payment run?" This narrows ambiguity and shortens delay. The best scripts are polite but firm, structured to elicit commitment rather than excuse. The collections calendar, in this sense, is not only a record but a guide for behaviour.

There is also a cultural dimension. In many organisations, chasing payment carries a stigma, as if it were impolite or desperate. But when reframed as part of service quality—ensuring clarity, confirming expectations, maintaining rhythm—it becomes professional, not personal. Just as delivery teams take pride in hitting milestones, finance teams can take pride in securing timely receipts. It is a matter of reframing collections not as confrontation but as stewardship of the company's most vital resource: cash.

The microeconomics of DSO illustrate why this matters. If a firm with £10 million in annual revenue reduces its DSO from 60 days to 45 days, it liberates roughly £410,000 in working capital. That is not paper value; it is cash that can fund hiring, inventory, or marketing. The calendar, in this sense, is a tool of capital efficiency as much as operational hygiene. Shrinking DSO is not an accounting curiosity—it is an act of strategy.

Of course, tensions remain. Not all clients respond equally. Some wield their payment cycles as leverage, confident that vendors will accept delay rather than jeopardise the relationship. Others simply lack internal discipline. Here, the collections calendar becomes diagnostic: it shows which clients honour commitments and which erode trust. That knowledge informs pricing, contract terms, and even whether to continue the relationship. A client that perpetually delays payment is not just a nuisance; it is effectively extracting an interest-free loan from your business.

Yet there is a philosophical thread to all this: collections are about truth. Businesses often indulge in illusions of liquidity, convincing themselves that invoices represent real, near-term cash. But cash is not real until it clears. The calendar forces leaders to face this truth weekly, to look at the exact pace of receipts, and to act before liquidity becomes crisis. It punctures wishful thinking and replaces it with discipline.

The unresolved question is whether businesses will embrace this discipline before they are forced to. Will leaders build collections calendars when times are good, or only after a cash crunch has exposed their weakness? Will they treat the rhythm of receipts as part of the operating system, or as an afterthought? The companies that answer early, with discipline, will buy themselves resilience. The rest will continue to confuse paper for money—until the bank balance proves otherwise.

Scenario toggles — Add base, stretch, and storm toggles with clear triggers. Avoid "one forecast to rule them all". Prepare choices before they are forced. Make switching modes easy.

In early 2020, as news of a virus moving across continents began to unsettle markets, many companies clung to their annual forecasts as if they were lifeboats. Boards debated "wait and see" while spreadsheets remained untouched, projecting sales curves that no longer bore any resemblance to reality. Others, more agile, did something different: they flipped into alternate modes. For them, there was not one forecast, but three. A base case, tracking steady assumptions. A stretch case, should demand surge or unexpected opportunity arise. And a storm case, spelling out what survival would look like under severe contraction. These firms had rehearsed their responses before crisis struck; when the world changed, they did not lose time deciding whether to cut, expand, or pivot. They switched modes.

This contrast captures the heart of scenario toggles. Businesses often behave as if a single forecast can serve all seasons, as if future uncertainty can be compressed into one neat line. But reality does not bend to spreadsheets. Markets swing, supply chains falter, costs spike, or customer demand collapses without notice. The question is not whether forecasts will be wrong—they will—but whether leaders will be paralysed when forced to adjust. A company without toggles is a company condemned to improvise when the stakes are highest.

A toggle-based approach acknowledges volatility as structural, not exceptional. Rather than pretending that one model can hold all truth, it builds three modes with explicit triggers: the baseline scenario, a stretch scenario, and a storm scenario. Each is linked to clear markers—conversion rates, cash balances, pipeline health, or macro signals. When a trigger is reached, the switch is immediate, removing hesitation. This turns scenario planning from abstract storytelling into operational choreography.

The base case is the practical default. It grounds the business in what is most likely, incorporating known variables and recent history. It is where teams plan weekly activity and resource allocation. But by itself, it breeds complacency. Without alternatives, leaders can be lulled into thinking that current trends will always hold.

The stretch case provides ambition. It sets a higher line for demand, revenue, or capacity, ensuring that opportunity does not catch the organisation flat-footed. Many businesses fail not because they miss upside, but because they cannot scale fast enough when upside appears. A stretch scenario forces preparation: if orders doubled in three months, how would we meet them? Which hires or capital would be required? Which bottlenecks would emerge?

The storm case is the most uncomfortable—and therefore the most necessary. It lays out the emergency script: how to shrink, protect liquidity, or reconfigure operations if revenues collapse or costs surge. Without a storm plan, leaders often delay difficult decisions until the bank account forces them, by which time the choices are fewer and harsher. A storm case, documented and rehearsed, is an act of self-respect: it allows a business to act before panic erodes clarity.

Clarity of triggers makes toggles powerful. It is not enough to vaguely sketch "if things go badly." Leaders must define the threshold: if cash falls below £250,000, the storm plan activates. If conversion rates exceed 25%, switch to stretch hiring. These triggers convert judgment into protocol, preventing endless debate when conditions shift. The process is less about predicting the future than about pre-deciding responses.

The psychology here is revealing. Humans dislike abandoning plans; we cling to prior assumptions even when evidence piles against them. Scenario toggles break this bias by formalising the switch. They transform "should we act?" into "the condition has been met; therefore, we act." This reduces paralysis and builds confidence. Employees, too, draw reassurance: they know the company has rehearsed both upside and downside, and that decisions will not be improvised at midnight in a crisis.

Examples abound. Consider a retailer whose base case forecast projected steady holiday sales. Its stretch case outlined the inventory, staff, and logistics needed if demand exceeded expectations. Its storm case detailed a 20% fall in consumer spending. When a supply chain shock hit, the storm case triggered automatically: the company froze hiring, shifted marketing spend, and renegotiated supplier terms. Meanwhile, a competitor—still operating on a single rosy forecast—burned through cash and entered administration.

The elegance of toggles lies in their simplicity. They do not require dozens of models or endless "what-if" permutations. They require three disciplined modes and the courage to assign thresholds. Complexity is replaced by readiness. Leadership meetings become sharper: rather than debating whether to believe in the forecast, teams discuss whether the trigger for switching has been reached.

There is, however, a deeper philosophical insight: scenario toggles are about humility. They admit that we cannot see the future clearly, that reality may take a path beyond our comfort zone. They embody intellectual honesty—acknowledging the limits of foresight while preparing practical responses. They allow leaders to balance optimism with prudence, to see opportunity without naivety, and to face risk without denial.

Yet an unresolved challenge remains. Will leaders adopt toggles before the next crisis, or will they continue to bet everything on the illusion of a single forecast? Preparedness demands effort and discipline—qualities easily postponed in the rush of daily work. The choice, then, is stark: build toggles while calm, or improvise when chaos arrives. The companies that choose the former will not only endure volatility—they will master it. The rest will discover, too late, that one forecast is never enough.

Reconcile and learn — Reconcile forecast to actuals weekly. Capture reasons for variance as learning. Turn misses into better models. Close the loop without blame.

Every ambitious plan looks flawless in its infancy. Forecasts hum with neat curves, revenues rise in steady increments, costs march in predictable lines, and cash balances glide along as if guided by destiny. Then reality intrudes. A client delays signing. A supplier misses a shipment. A marketing campaign underperforms. A tax bill arrives earlier than expected. Suddenly the elegant model diverges from the bank statement, and the spreadsheet loses its authority. It is in this gap—between projection and actuality—that the fate of many companies is determined.

The paradox is stark: forecasts are essential, yet they are always wrong. This is not a failure of intelligence, but the nature of foresight. The discipline is not in crafting a perfect forecast, but in systematically learning from its imperfection. To reconcile forecast to actuals each week is to face this gap head-on, to treat it not as embarrassment but as data. In doing so, leaders trade illusion for insight and build models that evolve with reality rather than resist it.

Consider the aviation industry. Every flight plan is written before take-off, mapping altitude, speed, fuel, and timing. Yet no pilot expects to follow it exactly. Winds shift, storms appear, and traffic control intervenes. Pilots do not see divergence as failure; they adjust course while continuously cross-checking against instruments. Businesses, by contrast, often cling to their initial forecast with religious fervour, treating variance as blameworthy rather than instructive. The result is denial until cash runs short.

A disciplined weekly reconciliation prevents such blindness. It requires three simple but radical acts: match the forecast to the actuals, capture the reasons for variance, and feed those lessons back into the model. Done consistently, this process transforms the forecast from a static artefact into a living system. It ceases to be a false prophecy and becomes a feedback engine.

The mechanics are straightforward. Begin with the forecasted line items: sales receipts, supplier payments, payroll, tax, rent. Compare them against the bank feed or ledger. Where the forecast and actual diverge, note it without judgement. Did a customer pay later than promised? Did expenses bunch differently across weeks? Did the team overestimate conversion rates or underestimate refund requests? Each variance is not a failure but a teacher.

Yet the deeper challenge is cultural. In many organisations, reconciliation devolves into finger-pointing. A missed sales number is blamed on the team; a delayed payment is pinned on operations. Such blame poisons the very process, encouraging people to hide or rationalise misses rather than explain them. A healthier culture treats misses as data, not indictments. Leaders must ask, *what is this variance teaching us about our assumptions?* rather than, *who is at fault?*

Case studies illustrate the power of this mindset. A subscription start-up noticed a recurring gap between forecast and actual receipts. On paper, invoices were due on the first of the month; in practice, most clients paid on the 12th or later. By reconciling weekly, the team realised their "due date" assumption was wishful fiction. They changed billing structures, added automated reminders, and within a quarter had reduced their days sales outstanding by ten days. The reconciliation did not simply adjust the forecast—it reshaped operations.

Another company, a small manufacturer, repeatedly missed its break-even target. Weekly reconciliation revealed a subtle pattern: small overruns in material costs, each insignificant alone, accumulated across product lines into a consistent drag. By surfacing these micro-variances, the team renegotiated supplier terms and redesigned packaging, recovering several points of margin. Without reconciliation, these hidden leaks would have remained submerged.

There is also a philosophical depth here. To reconcile forecast and actuals is to acknowledge fallibility without shame. It is a discipline in intellectual honesty: admitting that our models are simplifications, that reality contains surprises, and that progress lies not in defending our projections but in refining them. It requires humility, patience, and rigour—the qualities that separate durable businesses from fragile ones.

Weekly cadence matters. Monthly or quarterly reconciliation is too slow; the lag allows problems to compound and lessons to evaporate. Weekly review keeps the learning fresh, embedding it in the rhythm of operations. It also reduces emotional weight: small misses are easier to discuss openly than catastrophic surprises. Over time, the team internalises that forecasts are not commandments but hypotheses—always tested, always revised.

The act of capturing variance reasons is itself transformative. A simple annotation—"client delayed contract approval," "supplier invoiced early," "campaign response below target"—builds a database of lived experience. Over months, these notes form a pattern library, revealing systemic issues and recurring biases. Do we habitually overestimate customer speed? Underestimate regulatory friction? Such insights make future models sharper and decisions less naive.

The final step—feeding lessons back into the model—closes the loop. This is where reconciliation becomes learning. Without this, the process degenerates into a ritual of tallying misses. With it, the model evolves. Forecasts stop being static sheets and become iterative instruments, akin to pilots updating their flight path with each gust of wind.

But an unresolved tension remains. Even with reconciliation, variance never vanishes. The future remains stubbornly resistant to perfect modelling. The task is not to eliminate variance, but to cultivate resilience in its face—to build a culture where forecasts are constantly honed, where misses are mined for wisdom, and where the organisation moves with agility rather than rigidity. The question for any leader is simple yet profound: will you treat the gap between forecast and actuals as failure to be hidden, or as truth to be harnessed?

The companies that embrace the latter will find themselves learning faster than competitors, transforming uncertainty into advantage. Those that cling to denial or blame will discover, too late, that their numbers lied not because the world betrayed them, but because they refused to listen to what reality was teaching all along.

Chapter 7
Scenarios and Triggers

History is full of moments when the difference between collapse and survival was not brilliance but preparation. In 1962, during the Cuban Missile Crisis, the world stood on the edge of nuclear war. Both superpowers had stockpiled weapons and drawn red lines, but what mattered most in those days was not force—it was foresight. The quiet success of crisis management lay in rehearsed scenarios, pre-agreed thresholds, and the discipline to act on them without hesitation. Businesses, though their stakes are less apocalyptic, face a similar reality: in the fog of uncertainty, it is not improvisation that saves them, but pre-commitment.

The paradox is striking. Leaders often imagine their value lies in decisiveness under pressure, yet the most resilient organisations are those that make their decisions *before* the storm hits. It is not the frantic boardroom debate in the week cash runs short that decides survival, but the scenario mapped calmly six months earlier. In other words, clarity is not born in the heat of battle; it is designed in advance, when minds are cool and numbers are honest.

In practice, this means treating the future not as a single road but as a branching tree of possibilities. A new hire might accelerate growth or strain payroll. A change in payment terms might conserve cash or repel customers. A price increase might fatten margins or dampen demand. To navigate these forks, leaders must shift the conversation from opinion—what feels right, who shouts loudest—to consequence. What is the cash outcome if conversion rates slip? What happens if debtor days stretch? By mapping choices directly to numbers, argument turns into analysis, and rhetoric gives way to reality.

Yet building scenarios is not enough. One must also ask: what fragile assumptions underpin them? Here lies the discipline of the pre-mortem. Instead of celebrating a strategy's promise, the team imagines it has failed and asks why. This reversal surfaces hidden risks: the supplier who has no redundancy, the sales pipeline built on a single account, the product launch tied to a regulatory approval that may never come. To document these vulnerabilities, assign owners, and rehearse mitigations is not pessimism—it is prudence. It reduces the sting of surprise, turning the unknown into the merely difficult.

Still, knowing where danger lies does little if leaders hesitate when it arrives. That is why scenarios must be bound to triggers: hard thresholds that convert talk into action. Cash falling below a set reserve. Days sales outstanding stretching past an agreed point. Conversion rates dropping below a floor. These triggers act as numeric tripwires, removing dithering when anxiety clouds judgement. The best teams make such thresholds visible—on dashboards, in weekly meetings—and bind themselves to obey them. Discipline replaces wishful thinking, and hesitation gives way to pre-planned response.

But numbers alone do not lead. Scenarios and triggers are only effective if they are communicated beyond the executive suite. Staff must understand not just today's plan but tomorrow's contingencies. Suppliers must know the terms of engagement if storms arrive. Lenders, too, are reassured by transparency; they extend patience to those who show foresight rather than concealment. The art is to communicate futures without fear—framing them not as doom but as readiness. Done well, it builds trust: employees know what is coming, partners see reliability, and all stakeholders recognise that uncertainty has been met with clarity.

The tension, of course, never disappears. No tree of scenarios can anticipate every branch; no threshold can capture every nuance. The world always has surprises left. Yet the discipline of design, pre-mortem, trigger, and communication shifts the balance. It transforms uncertainty from paralysis into preparation, from threat into navigable terrain.

The question for every leader, then, is simple yet uncomfortable: will you wait to decide until the crisis forces your hand, or will you have already decided—quietly, soberly, with numbers as your guide—what must be done? The chapters ahead will argue that the difference is not abstract. It is survival. It is trust. It is the line between companies that crumble at the first gust of uncertainty and those that bend, adjust, and endure.

Design the decision tree — Map choices under uncertainty and link to cash outcomes. Move debate from opinion to consequence. Include price, hiring, terms, and product options. Keep the tree lightweight and live.

When the Apollo 13 mission famously declared, "Houston, we've had a problem," the hours that followed were not governed by debate but by disciplined options analysis. Engineers laid out branching pathways: if oxygen reserves fall this low, then this action follows; if voltage drops below this threshold, then that circuit must be cut. In the haze of crisis, clarity emerged not from inspired speeches but from decision trees already in the engineers' minds. The stakes were survival in space, yet the same principle holds on earth: under uncertainty, leaders cannot afford to argue from instinct or hierarchy. They must map choices to consequences—explicitly, transparently, and in cash terms.

The paradox of business decision-making is that many of the most consequential choices are taken in the fog of incomplete information. Should the company hire ahead of demand or wait until growth is proven? Should prices be raised despite customer pushback, or held flat to protect volume? Should a new product line be launched, knowing it will stretch working capital, or deferred until margins improve? In too many boardrooms, these questions devolve into opinion contests—extroverts dominate, anecdotes masquerade as data, and the loudest voice carries the day. A decision tree dismantles this theatre. It converts speculation into structured consequence: if we raise price by 5 per cent, then gross contribution rises by X, churn risk increases by Y, and cash runway extends or shortens accordingly.

At its heart, the decision tree is not an elaborate statistical model. It is a map—lightweight, live, and legible. Each branch links directly to financial outcomes, especially cash. By simplifying to consequence, the tool disciplines debate. Hiring is no longer "we need more capacity" versus "we must stay lean." It becomes: hiring two engineers at £60,000 each reduces cash runway by four months but shortens delivery cycles by 30 days. Now the trade-off is explicit, the decision tangible.

Consider the pricing lever. Many firms resist raising prices out of fear—fear of customer backlash, fear of lost deals, fear of reputational harm. Yet a decision tree reframes the choice. Map the scenario: if price increases by 5 per cent and volume drops by 2 per cent, contribution rises by £X. If volume drops by 10 per cent, contribution falls by £Y. Such mapping shows where the cliff edges truly lie. More often than not, the tree reveals that the risk is smaller than the myth; modest price increases often strengthen rather than weaken survival. Anchoring price debates in consequence, not conjecture, builds courage.

Payment terms provide another fertile ground. A decision tree can lay out the impact of shifting from net-60 to net-30 invoicing. If clients accept, cash inflow accelerates, days sales outstanding shrink, and the company gains weeks of runway. If pushback emerges, perhaps a discount-for-early-payment branch is added. Each option branches again—revenue preserved with discount, margin partially eroded, but cash stabilised. The organisation sees not abstract "better terms" but quantifiable trade-offs, each tied to survival.

Product choices, too, benefit from this mapping. A microbrewery weighing the launch of a seasonal stout, for instance, must consider not only projected sales but inventory strain, storage costs, and marketing overhead. The decision tree reveals paths: branch A shows a modest launch with limited kegs, reducing fixed cost exposure. Branch B pursues a national rollout, stretching capital and distribution. Each path leads to a cash outcome. The tree does not eliminate uncertainty, but it reframes it: uncertainty becomes a series of quantified paths rather than a fog of possibilities.

Crucially, the tree must remain lightweight. A 300-cell spreadsheet with dense macros paralyses more than it guides. What matters is agility: the ability to sketch, adjust, and revisit as conditions change. The tree must be live—updated weekly or monthly, responsive to real signals, adaptable without re-engineering. Leaders need to see the branches not as predictions carved in stone but as living possibilities, pruned or extended as reality unfolds.

The deeper philosophical point is this: decision trees embody humility. They admit that the future is plural, not singular; that no leader, however seasoned, can foresee the path with certainty. By laying out branches in advance, they prepare the organisation not for one world but for several, shifting smoothly as reality selects. In this sense, a decision tree is less about prediction than about preparation. It does not tell us which branch will occur; it tells us what we will do if it does.

But one tension remains unresolved. Even with a tree in hand, leaders often hesitate at the branch point itself. They may know the consequence of hiring, pricing, or product expansion, yet balk at committing. The question, then, is whether the discipline of mapping can overcome the inertia of fear. Can organisations learn not only to see their options but to choose, swiftly and without regret, when the trigger arrives? That, ultimately, is the test of whether decision trees remain diagrams on paper or become instruments of survival in practice.

Pre-mortem discipline — Run a pre-mortem to surface fragile assumptions. Document risks and mitigations with owners. Reduce surprise through rehearsal. Institutionalise candour.

In 1979, NASA lost its $125 million Orbiter due to a simple but devastating oversight: one engineering team had worked in metric units, another in imperial. No one caught the discrepancy until the spacecraft slammed into the Martian atmosphere. The post-mortem concluded that better systems could have prevented the disaster. Yet the tragedy was not inevitable. If a *pre*-mortem had been run—if the team had asked, *imagine this mission fails: why did it fail?*—the blind spot may have surfaced before it destroyed the project. The irony is clear: we conduct autopsies after the fact, but the discipline lies in imagining failure before it arrives.

The pre-mortem begins with a paradox: to protect a venture's survival, leaders must first envision its death. This is not cynicism, but courage. It asks participants to imagine themselves six months or a year from now, looking back on failure. What went wrong? Was it over-reliance on a single supplier? Overconfidence in customer uptake? A debt covenant breach triggered by an unanticipated dip in revenue? By flipping perspective from defensive optimism to retrospective realism, the exercise frees people to voice uncomfortable truths without being seen as pessimists or disloyal. Candour becomes sanctioned. The future is reframed not as a glossy pitch, but as a rehearsal for fragility.

In small businesses and start-ups, the need for pre-mortem discipline is even sharper than in space programmes. Capital is thinner, margins narrower, resilience shorter. A misplaced assumption—that a client will pay on time, that a campaign will deliver leads, that a key hire will stay—can unravel months of effort. The value of the pre-mortem lies in making these assumptions explicit, then testing them under stress. Which are fragile? Which have buffers? Which require immediate contingency plans? By documenting risks with named owners and proposed mitigations, the business builds a living risk map. When reality deviates, the organisation already knows who acts, how, and when.

Consider a young software firm planning to double its engineering headcount. In the optimism of growth, leaders assume funding will continue, sales will ramp, and attrition will stay low. A pre-mortem session reframes the outlook: imagine six months ahead, the firm is out of cash. Why? Perhaps the funder pulled out, sales cycles lengthened, or a competitor released a superior product. Each failure mode is then linked to a mitigation: diversifying investors, tightening payment terms, or accelerating a secondary revenue line. Documenting these with owners does not eliminate uncertainty, but it shrinks its sting. Surprises become rehearsed outcomes, not existential shocks.

The real challenge is cultural. Most organisations celebrate positivity and punish doubt. Meetings are filled with optimistic projections, while scepticism is dressed up as "resistance to change." A pre-mortem turns this norm upside down. It legitimises dissent, even demands it. The more uncomfortable the insight, the more valuable it is. A sales director admitting that key customers are habitually late payers, or a CTO acknowledging the fragility of the tech stack, is no longer undermining morale but strengthening resilience. The discipline institutionalises candour. Done repeatedly, it reshapes the culture: truth-telling becomes routine, not heroic exception.

The philosophical insight here is that fragility is not the enemy—it is blindness to fragility that destroys. Every venture carries weak points, but only those recognised can be reinforced. A pre-mortem functions as intellectual honesty under pressure: it refuses to mistake silence for safety or optimism for certainty. Instead, it confronts the inevitability of surprise, and by rehearsing failure, reduces its sting. The rehearsal becomes the safeguard.

Still, tension remains. Pre-mortems can identify a thousand risks, yet resources are finite. Which do you prepare for? Which do you tolerate? Which do you ignore? To run a pre-mortem is to confront not just fragility but prioritisation—the uncomfortable art of deciding which possible deaths to guard against and which to accept as unlikely but tolerable. This unresolved question ensures that the practice remains not mechanical but profoundly human. For even the best rehearsals cannot eliminate surprise; they can only prepare us to face it with steadier hands and clearer eyes.

Trigger thresholds — Set numeric tripwires for action: cash, DSO, conversion. Reduce dithering in stressful weeks. Make thresholds visible on the dashboard. Obey them.

In October 2008, as global markets convulsed, many businesses hesitated. The signs were clear—credit was tightening, orders slowing, invoices stretching—but decisions lagged behind reality. By the time leaders reacted, the cash had already bled out. What crippled them was not ignorance of the numbers but paralysis in the face of them. They had information but no triggers. In crisis, the absence of predetermined thresholds left decisions to nerves, personalities, and politics. The businesses that survived had a different discipline: they had already drawn their lines in the sand. When the dashboard flashed red, action followed automatically.

The paradox is stark: the more stressful the environment, the less capable humans are of rational judgement. Under pressure, we rationalise, delay, or cling to hope. Yet finance, unlike morale or strategy, is merciless to dithering. When cash dips below a safe buffer, every day of hesitation compounds risk. Trigger thresholds are designed to strip hesitation from decision-making. They are numeric tripwires that convert abstract uncertainty into explicit action. Drop below three weeks of cash runway? Freeze discretionary hiring. Watch Days Sales Outstanding extend past 75? Shift customer conversations from courtesy to collection. Conversion rate falls below 20%? Pause campaign spend until messaging is reset. Numbers become not just metrics but commands.

Designing these thresholds is both technical and philosophical. The technical task lies in choosing the right indicators—cash runway, DSO, conversion ratios, gross margin. Each must be defined precisely, measured consistently, and tracked in real time. The philosophical task lies in choosing courage over comfort: agreeing in advance that when the tripwire is triggered, action will be taken without delay. This is harder than it sounds. Leaders are tempted to override thresholds with "context" or "intuition." But the point of thresholds is to avoid precisely this temptation—to protect the firm from its own optimism bias in moments of strain.

A small manufacturing company provides a telling example. For years, its leaders had known that late payments were eroding liquidity. Yet every quarter, when DSO spiked, they deferred tough calls—fearing to alienate customers. It was only after codifying a trigger—that invoices beyond 60 days must automatically move to a senior collections call—that cash flow stabilised. The numbers were not new; the discipline was. The trigger threshold converted awareness into behaviour, protecting the firm not from external shocks but from internal reluctance.

This discipline extends beyond collections. Triggers can govern hiring, marketing spend, capital commitments, even product launches. A tech start-up, for example, might predefine that new hires in non-revenue roles are paused if net burn exceeds £150,000 for two consecutive months. Such clarity liberates managers: decisions are no longer personal battles but pre-agreed consequences. The conversation shifts from *should we act?* to *the condition has been met; now we act.* The language of inevitability disarms debate.

The visibility of thresholds is as important as their existence. Hidden in a spreadsheet or buried in a CFO's notebook, they lose their force. Placed on a dashboard—seen weekly by executives, managers, sometimes even frontline staff—they become cultural. Everyone learns the firm's vital signs, everyone sees when the numbers approach danger, and everyone knows what happens next. Transparency builds trust: staff understand that decisions are not arbitrary, that pauses or cuts are not whims but pre-committed responses. For lenders and suppliers, too, visible thresholds are reassuring. They show discipline, foresight, and the ability to act before crisis rather than after it.

Yet here lies the enduring tension: thresholds demand obedience, but reality is always more nuanced. What if cash dips because of a one-off delay that resolves tomorrow? What if DSO is skewed by a single large client who always pays late but never defaults? To obey thresholds blindly is to risk rigidity; to ignore them is to invite chaos. The art is not in eliminating this tension but in acknowledging it. Triggers should be designed with buffers, not hair-triggers; with room for professional judgement, but without the comfort of endless deferral.

At its heart, the practice of trigger thresholds is a recognition of human limits. We are bad at making hard calls in moments of fear. We are worse at admitting this to ourselves. Thresholds, like guardrails on a mountain road, are not there to replace judgement but to prevent catastrophe when judgement falters. They convert abstract financial drift into concrete signals, and they force the organisation to act before circumstances make acting irrelevant.

The unresolved question remains: how many tripwires can a business live with before it strangles its own flexibility? Too few, and dithering returns; too many, and adaptability is lost. That balance is never settled once and for all. Each firm must redraw its thresholds as it grows, as markets shift, as risk appetites change. What matters most is not perfection but commitment: a willingness to live by the numbers when they tell us what we least want to hear. The courage is not in setting the trigger but in obeying it when it snaps.

Communicating futures — Explain scenarios to staff, suppliers, and lenders. Use transparency to create alignment. Avoid fear with clear contingencies. Build trust with numbers.

When Franklin Roosevelt told Americans in 1933 that "the only thing we have to fear is fear itself," he was doing more than offering comfort—he was performing a feat of communication under extreme uncertainty. Banks were failing, unemployment was spiralling, and yet his words turned panic into resolve. What mattered was not certainty—none was possible—but clarity about the landscape of risk, the actions being taken, and the role each citizen played in recovery. The principle endures: in moments of financial fragility, what leaders communicate—and how—shapes not just confidence but survival.

Businesses today face their own versions of that moment. A delayed receivable, a sharp fall in demand, a sudden supply chain squeeze—each can trigger cascading anxiety inside and outside the organisation. Left unaddressed, silence breeds rumour, and rumour corrodes trust. Staff imagine redundancies, suppliers fear defaults, lenders prepare for losses. The paradox is that in trying to protect stakeholders from bad news, leaders often make matters worse. Vagueness invites speculation; opacity fuels dread. What creates stability is not the pretence of control but the discipline of communicating futures.

At its heart, communicating futures means giving form to uncertainty. It involves presenting scenarios—base, stretch, and storm—not as predictions but as structured possibilities. When staff know that if revenues fall 20% a hiring freeze will follow, or when suppliers see that payment terms are secured under defined conditions, anxiety is replaced by comprehension. Fear thrives on ambiguity; numbers cut it down to size. The act of scenario-sharing transforms potential chaos into navigable terrain.

Consider the case of a mid-sized engineering firm during the pandemic. Orders collapsed in the spring of 2020, and leadership faced the temptation to issue bland reassurances. Instead, they convened their teams and suppliers with three explicit forecasts: a base case of 60% revenue retention, a stretch case of 80%, and a storm case of 40%. Each came with spelled-out contingencies—reduced shifts, deferred capital expenditure, renegotiated credit lines. The honesty was bracing, but it aligned everyone. Staff tightened efficiency knowing what was at stake; suppliers extended terms knowing repayment was mapped; lenders extended facilities knowing defaults were not being hidden but planned for. Transparency did not prevent difficulty, but it prevented collapse.

This approach challenges a common managerial instinct: the fear that disclosing scenarios will demoralise. In fact, the opposite is more often true. People fear the unknown more than the unpleasant. When numbers are hidden, every employee fills the void with their own worst-case imagination. By contrast, when leadership says, *if cash falls below £500,000, here is what we will do,* employees grasp both the risk and the remedy. The result is not despair but agency: individuals see where their efforts can influence outcomes, and stakeholders grasp how their cooperation matters.

But communication must be precise. Vague statements like "we are monitoring the situation" or "we expect improvement soon" are worse than silence. They sound evasive, and they erode credibility. Effective communication requires tying futures to quantifiable triggers: *when DSO exceeds 70 days, collections escalate; when conversion dips below 15%, marketing pauses; when burn rate exceeds plan by 10%, hiring halts.* Such clarity is not only operationally useful—it is morally respectful. It treats staff and partners as adults capable of handling conditional truth rather than as children in need of reassurance.

There is, however, a delicate balance between transparency and panic. Numbers must be framed with contingencies, not left as naked threats. Saying "if revenues fall by 30%, we will have to cut staff" sparks fear; saying "if revenues fall by

30%, here are three steps we will take first—reducing discretionary spend, renegotiating leases, and pausing recruitment—before redundancies are considered" creates confidence that leadership has thought beyond the bluntest tool. It is the difference between fear and trust.

The wider implication is that communicating futures institutionalises candour. It forces leaders to expose their own assumptions, to articulate thresholds, and to confront uncomfortable possibilities in advance. A lender who hears not just projections but the rules for when projections fail is far more likely to extend credit. A supplier who sees their client wrestling openly with scenarios is more likely to stay loyal through lean months. Transparency, when coupled with action plans, is not weakness but currency.

Yet unresolved tensions remain. How much should a leader share without overwhelming people? When does transparency become noise? At what point does detail stop building trust and start eroding confidence? These are questions without permanent answers. What matters most is intent: whether communication is designed to control perception or to create alignment. Stakeholders can smell the difference. One breeds cynicism, the other earns loyalty.

To communicate futures is to accept responsibility for uncertainty. It does not mean eliminating doubt—it means translating it into shared frameworks, numbers, and contingencies. The organisation ceases to be a crowd of individuals guessing in the dark and becomes a collective that knows what will happen when the dials move. The test of leadership lies not in producing certainty but in building trust strong enough to withstand its absence. And so the lingering question is this: when the next shock arrives—and it will—will your people be bracing for the unknown, or standing ready with the map you have already drawn?

Chapter 8
Collections and Terms That Stick

In 2008, as credit markets froze, small businesses across Europe discovered a brutal truth: profitability meant little if customers did not pay on time. Firms with healthy order books collapsed, not from lack of demand, but from delayed receipts. The pain was not abstract. It meant founders taking out personal loans to cover payroll, suppliers cutting ties when invoices languished unpaid, and otherwise sound companies shuttering simply because cash did not arrive fast enough. It was a reminder that business is not sustained by promises written on invoices, but by money in the bank.

The paradox is obvious yet often ignored: companies devote vast resources to winning sales, negotiating contracts, and delivering products, but treat the act of getting paid as an afterthought—an administrative tail rather than a strategic head. In truth, collections and terms are as fundamental as pricing or cost control. They shape not only cash flow but also trust, resilience, and the ability to invest in growth. A company can survive thin margins longer than it can survive late payments. Cash starvation is swifter and more unforgiving than erosion of profit.

Behind every delayed payment sits a human interaction. A polite but firm reminder within 48 hours often secures funds that a month of silence cannot. A client may delay not out of malice but out of competing priorities or bureaucratic inertia. The speed and tone of the first contact matters because it signals seriousness. Ignore it, and you invite a new hierarchy in which your invoice becomes the easiest to postpone. Confront it constructively, and you set expectations that shape the entire relationship. Payment behaviour, like most behaviour, is moulded by habit and consequence.

Collections, then, are not a mechanical exercise in chasing numbers. They are a dialogue between people, coloured by psychology, status, and respect. The companies that collect well are those that embed humanity into the process: reminders that are insistent without being abrasive, scripts that show empathy for difficulties while remaining anchored in clarity, and systems that make payment effortless rather than cumbersome. A client asked to print, sign, and fax a form is more likely to delay than one offered a secure one-click payment link. Cash flow is lubricated by convenience as much as by pressure.

There is also architecture beneath the human layer: the structure of terms themselves. Deposits, retainers, and milestone payments are not merely contractual devices; they are cash defences. They shift the balance of risk from the supplier to the buyer, ensuring that production capacity is never fully exposed without compensation. A builder who secures staged payments protects their workforce and materials; a consultant who insists on a retainer ensures continuity of effort without the corrosive anxiety of unpaid hours. Terms, when designed intelligently, alter not just the timing of cash but the psychology of obligation. They make clear that value is delivered in tandem with payment, not in hope of it.

Yet friction is inevitable. Disputes and deductions surface, sometimes legitimate, sometimes as stalling tactics. The difference lies in design: an organisation with a light, well-signposted dispute process can isolate real issues quickly and keep the majority of cash flowing. Without it, every minor query metastasises into an excuse for non-payment. Closing loops fast, distinguishing genuine defects from dilatory behaviour, and resolving with fairness but firmness—these are not administrative details but survival practices.

The significance of collections and terms extends beyond the balance sheet. They signal discipline to staff, seriousness to clients, and credibility to financiers. A lender, when assessing a company, looks less at revenue growth than at how reliably that revenue converts into cash. Suppliers judge not only on how orders are placed, but on how they are honoured financially. Employees, too, draw cues: a business that collects consistently is a business that can pay consistently. Reliability in receipts underwrites reliability in wages, investments, and morale.

And yet a question lingers, provocative in its simplicity: why do so many leaders flinch at treating collections as strategy? Why do they rehearse sales pitches endlessly but send out payment reminders with embarrassment, as if collecting were beneath them? Perhaps it is cultural—the discomfort of mixing money with relationships. Perhaps it is denial—the hope that avoiding awkward conversations will somehow produce cash. Whatever the cause, the effect is universal: companies that fail to master collections end up negotiating from weakness, beholden to the timing of others.

This chapter invites a shift in perspective. Collections and terms are not footnotes to finance; they are the backbone of resilience. They determine whether growth is fuelled or strangled, whether opportunities are seized or missed, and whether relationships are built on mutual respect or quiet exploitation. The aim is not to chase money aggressively but to design processes and behaviours that make payment natural, expected, and timely.

The payoff is profound: a business that knows its scripts, secures deposits, manages disputes with agility, and instils habits of prompt payment stands not only solvent but sovereign—able to steer rather than be dragged by circumstance. The question, then, is not whether you will get paid, but whether you will shape the terms of that payment with foresight and confidence—or leave them to chance. The answer to that question will often determine the line between survival and strength.

The psychology of getting paid — Design human follow-ups that are polite and persistent. Show why speed of first contact matters. Make paying easy. Turn relationships into timely cash.

A restaurant owner once said, "I don't mind people arguing about the bill, I mind when they forget it exists." His point was sharp: debts left unspoken too quickly turn invisible, and invisibility is the enemy of cash flow. In business, invoices are rarely unpaid because someone lost belief in their legitimacy. They are unpaid because of inertia, competing priorities, or a silent recalibration of what matters most in a busy day. The paradox is that money owed is most at risk of being ignored precisely when it is most assumed to be automatic.

It is tempting for business leaders to think of collecting money as mechanical—an invoice generated, a due date set, a transfer made. But money moves when people do, and people are not mechanical. They forget, they delay, they juggle, they avoid. Which means that the psychology of getting paid is as crucial as the process of issuing an invoice. Cash collection is, at its heart, about human behaviour. The best systems do not bully or berate; they make the act of paying visible, easy, and urgent, while maintaining the dignity of the relationship.

The speed of first contact after an invoice becomes overdue is more than administrative efficiency. It is a psychological marker. A polite, same-day nudge tells the payer that your invoice sits high on the priority list, that your organisation notices, and that delay carries consequence. A week of silence sends the opposite message: deferment is safe, perhaps even expected. Just as a teacher who ignores a late essay invites more lateness, a supplier who stays quiet trains customers that promptness is optional. Behaviour is shaped not by the rules in a contract but by the lived experience of reinforcement.

Consider two contractors. One sends a friendly reminder the morning after an invoice slips past due: "Just flagging this for your attention—we'd appreciate settlement this week so we can keep your project moving smoothly." The other waits three weeks, then sends a terse demand letter. Which one is more likely to be paid on time next month? The former, not because they are harsher, but because they are quicker, clearer, and more consistent. In payments, timeliness beats toughness.

Politeness is not weakness. Done properly, it strengthens the relationship. A message that recognises the client's busyness but holds firm on the obligation conveys professionalism rather than hostility. It shows that you value the partnership enough to maintain standards. Persistent but respectful follow-ups transform collections from awkward confrontation into steady expectation. They shift the dynamic from *"please do us a favour"* to *"this is how we work together."* In this light, collecting money is less about extracting funds than about teaching habits of reciprocity.

Ease matters too. Businesses often underestimate the friction in their own processes. A finance team that insists on paper cheques, manual forms, or obscure payment portals introduces drag that magnifies delay. A company that sends a secure payment link or sets up automatic debit reduces excuses and accelerates cash. Behavioural science tells us that people default to the path of least resistance. The question is: are you making payment the smooth path, or the stumbling one?

Technology helps, but tone still matters more. Automated reminders stripped of warmth risk alienating; equally, vague apologies for "bothering you" undermine confidence. The art lies in blending systems with humanity: a structured schedule of reminders that grow firmer over time, couched in language that balances empathy with expectation. For example: "We're sure this is an oversight—please let us know if there's an issue," followed by, "As per our terms, payment was due last week—please confirm processing today." The rhythm is steady, the escalation clear, the respect intact.

The psychology of getting paid is also about hierarchy. In most organisations, finance teams rank invoices against competing obligations: salaries, suppliers, rent. Those who follow up promptly and consistently rise to the top of that list. Those who stay silent sink. It is not malice but triage. In this sense, following up is not nagging—it is competing for attention in a crowded queue. The companies that collect best understand this and train their teams to treat follow-ups not as pleading but as professional prioritisation.

Relationships carry weight. Clients who trust you are more likely to pay you. But trust is not fostered by ignoring money; it is reinforced by clarity about it. The most enduring partnerships are those where both sides know the rules, honour them, and address lapses quickly. Awkwardness corrodes trust, while transparency builds it. A customer who feels respected in reminders is more likely to see payment not as a transaction but as a reflection of mutual reliability.

Yet a lingering question should keep leaders alert: if getting paid is so rooted in psychology, why do so many companies treat it as an afterthought, outsourced to generic email templates or left to junior staff with little training? Why do organisations invest in sales scripts but not in payment scripts? Perhaps it is cultural—an unease about mixing money with relationships. Perhaps it is structural—collections seen as back-office rather than front-line. Whatever the cause, the result is the same: preventable cash stress, solvency risks, and unnecessary strain.

The truth is simple, though uncomfortable: how you collect shapes how you are respected. A business that collects with speed, clarity, and grace teaches customers how to treat it. One that delays, apologises, or obfuscates teaches the opposite. In that sense, the psychology of getting paid is also the psychology of being taken seriously. The next time an invoice goes past due, the question is not only *how do we secure this payment?* but also *what habit are we teaching this customer for the future?* The answer will determine not just today's cash flow, but tomorrow's stability.

Scripts and sequences — Provide a 21-day email and call sequence. Start friendly, escalate firmly, and preserve respect. Include exact phrases that work. Track each touch.

A business leader once described late payments as "death by a thousand delays." None of the delays, taken alone, felt catastrophic: a client travelling, an accounts payable clerk changing roles, a cheque run moved to the next week. But together, they suffocated cash flow. The striking paradox is that most overdue payments are not disputes at all—they are drifts. And the only proven antidote to drift is rhythm: a sequence of touches so steady, respectful, and clear that inertia is dislodged before it turns into avoidance.

Why does sequence matter so much? Because payment is not just a financial act, but a behavioural one. Humans procrastinate. We respond to nudges, deadlines, and escalations that are predictable but polite. Just as a medical reminder service can raise prescription compliance by 30 per cent through consistent nudges, a structured follow-up sequence transforms receivables from fragile promises into actual cash. Without sequence, reminders are random; with sequence, they become habit—on both sides of the transaction.

The art lies in balance: firm enough to show seriousness, but courteous enough to preserve dignity. Too lenient, and the message is "you can pay when you like." Too aggressive, and trust collapses. Respectful persistence builds a subtle but powerful expectation: this company notices, this company follows up, this company deserves to be prioritised.

The most effective follow-up systems compress time. Research in collections consistently shows that the likelihood of payment drops sharply after the first week past due. A same-day or next-day reminder communicates not only efficiency but also fairness: you expect the terms to be respected, as they would expect from you. The initial tone is gentle, almost collegial: "We wanted to check if everything was received and in process—please let us know if you need any details from our side." It assumes goodwill while planting a clear flag.

By day seven, the message must be firmer but still cordial: "Our records show invoice #145 is now one week past due. Could you confirm processing by Friday? That will help us keep your project on track without interruption." The subtle shift is from inquiry to expectation. The wording points to consequence—not as threat, but as fact. Cash flow underpins continuity, and continuity serves both parties.

The second week is critical. This is when polite silence risks becoming tacit permission. The script must now add weight. A phone call, not just an email, brings human presence back into the exchange. A simple line—"I wanted to speak directly so we can get this cleared—when can we expect payment?"—cuts through delay more effectively than another email in a crowded inbox. Voice conveys seriousness that text cannot. Yet the tone remains professional, never desperate: the message is *we are partners, and partnership includes keeping agreements.*

By day fourteen, the sequence escalates. A message might read: "We value our relationship and want to avoid any disruption. Payment for invoice #145 was due two weeks ago—please confirm today when funds will be transferred." The emphasis is no longer on inquiry, but on resolution. Still, the respect remains intact: you acknowledge value, even as you hold the line.

As the third week begins, the tone must sharpen without collapsing into hostility. A day twenty-one contact can be both final and constructive: "Despite earlier reminders, invoice #145 remains unpaid. Unless we receive confirmation of payment this week, we may need to pause further work. We'd prefer to resolve this quickly together—please advise today." Here, consequence is no longer implied—it is stated. Yet even now, the phrasing offers an outstretched hand: a chance to resolve without damage.

The sequence works because it escalates naturally. The customer is never surprised, never blindsided. Each step is predictable, measured, and documented. And documentation matters: tracking every touch ensures that communication is not scattered or duplicated, and it provides a clear record should disputes ever escalate further. It also sharpens discipline within your own team—collections cannot depend on memory or goodwill alone.

This structured cadence also shifts the psychological frame. Customers who see a consistent pattern—email, call, reminder, escalation—learn to take deadlines seriously. They know what comes next. They adjust behaviour accordingly. In this way, the sequence does not just collect overdue invoices; it prevents future lateness. It sets a standard: promptness is normal, delays are noticed, consequences follow.

Critically, scripts must be written, not improvised. Polite persistence sounds effortless only when it is planned. Phrases like "please confirm processing today" or "we'd like to resolve this quickly together" blend firmness with cooperation. Contrast this with vague appeals such as "we'd appreciate payment soon," which invite procrastination. Precision in language signals precision in practice.

Some will argue that rigidity risks damaging relationships. In truth, the opposite is often found. Customers respect suppliers who are clear, consistent, and professional in handling money. Ambiguity breeds frustration; clarity breeds trust. By scripting and sequencing communication, you protect both your balance sheet and your reputation. You show that your company values both civility and seriousness.

Yet a question lingers: what does it say about us, culturally, that companies pour energy into chasing new sales but hesitate to invest equal craft in collecting what is already earned? Why do businesses rehearse pitches endlessly but neglect to rehearse follow-ups? Perhaps because asking for money feels uncomfortable, while asking for business feels aspirational. But the reality is that solvency depends more on collections than on charm. Respectful persistence is not merely operational—it is existential.

And so, scripts and sequences are more than tools for debt recovery. They are rituals of discipline. They turn cash flow into a living rhythm, where promises are noticed, timelines are honoured, and relationships are strengthened through clarity. The real question for any leader is not whether you *can* design such a system, but whether you are willing to adopt one—knowing that to do so is to confront not only your customers' habits, but your own.

Deposits, retainers, milestones — Operationalise upfronts and progress payments. Tie money to deliverables. Use real examples from services and construction. Reduce risk at the source.

A century-old lesson in business risk management lies hidden in the practices of construction contracts. No contractor pours concrete or lays brick without securing a deposit and a schedule of milestone payments. They understand, almost instinctively, that cash must march in step with work. A skyscraper is not built on promises—it is built on staged payments, each tied to tangible progress. And yet, in modern professional services, creative industries, and even technology ventures, many still embark on projects on little more than a handshake and a hope that invoices will be honoured weeks or months later.

The paradox is stark: the businesses least able to absorb non-payment—the small firm, the independent consultant, the cash-light start-up—are often the ones who work longest without securing upfront commitments. The psychology is understandable: fear of scaring away a client, a belief that trust must be granted in advance, or a misguided optimism that "they'll pay when they can." But optimism is not a strategy, and trust without structure leaves the fragile exposed. The true mark of professionalism is not in extending endless credit, but in designing terms that respect both sides and keep risk proportionate.

Deposits are the simplest and most powerful instrument for aligning commitment. A deposit transforms intent into obligation. It shifts the relationship from a conversation about possibilities to a contract with skin in the game. A consultant asking for 30 per cent upfront is not being difficult; they are ensuring that the client values the work enough to invest before it begins. This modest act filters out unserious enquiries, strengthens the supplier's bargaining position, and creates a financial anchor that reduces the temptation for the client to drift or delay.

Retainers operate on a similar principle, but extend it into continuity. They transform sporadic, unpredictable income into a steady baseline, often covering advisory or support services that ebb and flow over time. Law firms, marketing agencies, and IT providers have long used retainers to create predictability. The client benefits too: they secure priority access, faster responses, and ongoing support without renegotiating each time. What looks at first like a cautious hedge for the provider is, in reality, a structure that provides mutual stability.

Milestone payments, meanwhile, are the bridge between deposits and final settlement. They are most visible in construction—"payment on foundation completion, on framing, on roofing"—but they apply equally in less tangible fields. A software developer can tie payments to deliverables: design mock-ups, beta version, live deployment. A training provider can link instalments to module delivery. By structuring fees around progress, both parties share visibility and accountability: the supplier knows cash is coming, and the client knows progress is measurable.

The effect is transformative. Instead of a binary risk—paid in full or not at all—the business creates a series of checkpoints that de-risk the relationship. Each payment acts as a renewal of trust, a reaffirmation of momentum. Cash flow becomes less volatile, disputes are contained earlier, and the power imbalance between supplier and buyer is moderated.

Of course, objections arise. Some clients resist deposits or staged payments, arguing that they prefer to pay "on completion." The irony is that these same clients would never dream of demanding such terms from their builder, their lawyer, or their airline. You cannot board a plane and promise to pay only after you land safely. Framing the discussion in these terms often clarifies the point: staged or upfront payments are not about mistrust; they are about fairness, reciprocity, and operational prudence.

For the business leader, the challenge is not only to adopt deposits, retainers, and milestones, but to operationalise them—to embed them in contracts, proposals, and culture so that they cease to be awkward negotiations and become standard practice. Language matters: "to secure your project slot, we require a 25 per cent deposit," or "progress payments are tied to each completed stage of delivery." These phrases convey normality and professionalism, not suspicion. The goal is to make structured payments feel as natural as invoicing itself.

Consider the alternative: a design agency that delivers six weeks of work on a major campaign without a deposit, only to find the client has shifted priorities and delays payment indefinitely. Staff are still paid, rent is still due, but the firm is now financing the client's indecision. Contrast this with the agency that collects a deposit upfront and milestone instalments every two weeks. Their risk exposure is capped, their runway is preserved, and their client relationship is strengthened by clarity.

The wisdom here reaches beyond transactions. It is a philosophy of risk management: reduce exposure at the source rather than firefighting later. A deposit is not just cash in the bank; it is a symbolic act of mutual seriousness.

A retainer is not just steady revenue; it is a framework for enduring partnership. A milestone payment is not just an instalment; it is an agreement to pace trust with progress.

And yet, many hesitate. They fear that insisting on deposits or staged terms will deter business. The deeper truth is that clients who refuse any upfront structure often carry the greatest risk. Saying "yes" to such arrangements may feel like winning work, but it is often the start of losing control. The courage to insist on fair terms is not only financial discipline—it is strategic survival.

The question that lingers is whether businesses will continue to view deposits, retainers, and milestones as optional extras, or whether they will embrace them as foundational tools of professionalism. If construction firms have relied on them for centuries, why should modern service businesses leave themselves so exposed? To operationalise these practices is to stop gambling on goodwill and start building on structure. The decision is less about whether to ask, and more about whether you can afford not to.

Disputes and deductions — Build a light dispute process. Separate real issues from stalling tactics. Keep cash moving during resolution. Close loops fast.

In every business relationship, money owed is money contested until it is safely in the bank. History shows that the most perilous moments in commerce are rarely the dramatic bankruptcies but the quiet, grinding delays in payment—delays disguised as "clarifications," "adjustments," or "pending checks." A supplier may hear that an invoice is "under review" or that a "minor discrepancy" has halted release. Weeks pass. Cash dwindles. Staff are paid from reserves. The company begins financing not its own operations, but the indecision or avoidance of its customers.

The paradox is that disputes, real or contrived, thrive in the very businesses that cannot afford them. Small firms and contractors often operate with thinner margins, shorter runways, and less bargaining power. Yet it is precisely these firms that find themselves tied up in drawn-out back-and-forths over deductions, claims, or ambiguities in scope. Left unmanaged, disputes become a slow bleed: energy diverted into argument, time lost to endless correspondence, and liquidity eroded while the outcome remains uncertain.

A disciplined approach to disputes begins with acknowledging their dual nature. Some disputes are legitimate: a product arrives damaged, a service falls short of specification, an agreement leaves genuine ambiguity. These are moments for accountability, adjustment, and learning. But many disputes are not rooted in real substance. They are tactics—stalling to preserve cash on the buyer's side, exploiting vagueness to avoid prompt payment, or pushing blame to weaken the supplier's resolve. The craft lies in separating these two early, with a light but clear process that channels each to its appropriate resolution.

One of the most effective practices is to treat disputes as exceptions, not as reasons to suspend the entire cash flow. Instead of allowing a contested line item to freeze the entire invoice, firms should structure agreements so that uncontested amounts are paid immediately, while disputed items are isolated and addressed in parallel. This keeps cash moving and prevents a minor issue from paralysing the whole relationship. Construction contracts often embody this wisdom: interim payments continue even while specific claims are debated, preventing projects from grinding to a halt.

The process itself need not be heavy-handed. The goal is speed and clarity, not bureaucracy. A light dispute mechanism might follow three steps: rapid identification of the disputed element; designation of an owner on both sides to investigate; and a firm timeline—days, not weeks—for resolution. By documenting this process in contracts or terms of trade, businesses set expectations upfront. It signals to clients: disagreements will be dealt with, but they will not become indefinite excuses.

Consider a design agency that delivers campaign materials only to be told the final invoice is "too high compared to expectations." Without a process, this can spiral into vague debates, lost time, and withheld cash. With a documented system, however, the agency immediately separates the uncontested work from the disputed portion. Eighty per cent of the invoice is paid within days; the remaining twenty per cent is channelled into a short, structured review. The client still has space to voice concerns, but the supplier is not left financing their hesitation.

Speed is more than operational—it is psychological. The longer a dispute lingers, the more entrenched each side becomes, and the harder it is to untangle fact from posture. Fast loops keep candour alive. They make it easier for both sides to correct errors without embarrassment and to close matters while goodwill remains. Slowness, by contrast, corrodes trust, signalling either weakness or manipulation.

Behind this lies a deeper philosophy: disputes should be learning opportunities, not repeated wounds. By capturing the reasons behind legitimate deductions—unclear scoping, vague contracts, mismatched expectations—companies can improve their front-end processes and reduce recurrence. Each resolved dispute is not only a closed case but also an input into better contracting, clearer deliverables, and sharper communication. This reframes disputes from chronic liabilities into feedback loops that strengthen resilience.

And yet, candour in disputes requires courage. Too often, managers allow "client diplomacy" to blur into avoidance, letting weeks pass without decisive follow-up. The hard truth is that respectful persistence is not rudeness. It is a form of stewardship, safeguarding the business's ability to serve not only this client but all clients. A supplier paralysed by unpaid invoices may look polite on the surface but is quietly eroding its capacity to deliver.

The lightness of the dispute process matters as much as its firmness. Heavy legalistic structures invite defensiveness; they escalate small disagreements into adversarial battles. A transparent, time-bound, and proportionate process, by contrast, preserves relationships while protecting cash. It frames disputes not as crises but as structured conversations within agreed rules.

Still, the tension remains: what happens when the line between genuine dispute and stalling tactic blurs, when ambiguity is weaponised, when payment is stretched by design rather than accident? At what point does patience turn into complicity in your own exploitation? The unanswered question lingers—how far can professionalism bend before it must harden into refusal?

For businesses, the challenge is not simply to design dispute processes but to live them with discipline, refusing to let ambiguity or delay hollow out their resilience. The real test is not in the rare courtroom battle but in the dozens of small disputes that creep into everyday commerce. Whether these become slow leaks or quick corrections depends on whether firms build—and obey—structures that keep cash moving, even when agreement does not.

Chapter 9
Pick Your Capital, Keep Control

When Thomas Cook collapsed in 2019, a company with 178 years of history vanished almost overnight. Its balance sheet was burdened not only by mounting debt but also by unfavourable terms with suppliers and lenders. Holidaymakers stranded across the world became the visible story, but behind the headlines lay a quieter truth: when cash, capital, and control slip out of alignment, even the most established business can unravel. Cook did not run out of customers—it ran out of choices.

Every entrepreneur, whether leading a start-up or steering a family business, eventually faces the same stark question: where will the next pound come from, and what strings will it carry? The paradox is that while money fuels growth, it also shapes destiny. The wrong kind of capital, at the wrong time, can cost more than interest or equity—it can cost independence, timing, and even the right to steer one's own ship.

This chapter begins from a simple but often neglected starting point: before turning to outside investors or bankers, have you squeezed the capital already embedded within your operations? Working capital—the daily dance between receivables, payables, and stock—is the cheapest, fastest source of cash, and yet the most overlooked. A tightened collections rhythm, a renegotiated supplier term, or a leaner inventory cycle can yield more liquidity than a six-figure loan. The entrepreneur who masters working capital is not just raising cash; they are buying time, discipline, and bargaining power.

And yet, the capital conversation cannot stop there. Businesses must eventually weigh the great triad: debt, equity, and revenue-based finance. Each carries not only cost but cadence: loans bring covenants and schedules, equity brings partners and diluted control, revenue-share instruments flex with income but can quietly drain margins. The sharp operator does not chase "cheap money" alone but matches the instrument to the rhythm of their cash flows. To misalign is to invite strain; to align is to multiply resilience.

The art, however, is not merely in choosing but in negotiating. Bankers and lenders are not swayed by thick binders or glossy decks. They are moved by precision: a one-page packet that shows cycle discipline, debt coverage, and covenants a business can live with. Present like an anxious supplicant, and doors remain closed. Present like a calm, disciplined operator—one who knows their numbers and their limits—and the odds of a yes increase dramatically.

But even a successful raise brings responsibility. Capital is not oxygen to be inhaled until it disappears; it is fuel, and fuel demands a flight plan. The most enduring companies articulate *use of proceeds* with the same clarity as a pilot's route map: what the money will buy, how it will return, and how progress will be tracked week by week. Drift after funding is the great silent killer of enterprises. The firms that thrive are those that prove their thesis with cash in motion, not with words on a pitch deck.

The stakes could not be higher. Pick the wrong capital, and you may gain resources at the expense of freedom. Pick no capital, and you may preserve control but starve growth. Navigate wisely, and you preserve both—the funds to act and the autonomy to act on your own terms. The question that hangs over every entrepreneur is therefore not just *how much* capital they need, but *what kind* they are willing to live with.

The following pages will not hand you universal answers, because there are none. Instead, they will sharpen your questions: How much hidden capital lies in your own cycle? Which clauses are red lines, even if a lender insists? How do you ensure that every borrowed or invested pound is tied to a visible return? In these questions lies the heart of business sovereignty—the ability to fund growth without ceding command.

Capital, after all, is not just arithmetic. It is governance. It is trust. It is the line between being a company that survives on its own terms and one that merely endures at the pleasure of others. The challenge is to master the instruments of finance without becoming mastered by them. And so we turn to the real work: choosing wisely, negotiating firmly, and, above all, keeping control.

Working capital first — Fix the cycle before raising. Show how terms improvements "raise" cash. Quantify impact versus loans. Choose the cheapest, fastest cash first.

When a small British manufacturer in the Midlands teetered on the edge of insolvency, its directors did what many business owners instinctively do: they rushed to the bank, hat in hand, to plead for a short-term loan. But as the firm's finance manager quietly demonstrated, the problem was not a lack of available capital; it was a cash cycle clogged by slow-paying customers and indulgent supplier terms. By renegotiating receivables from 60 to 30 days and stretching payables from 30 to 45, the company unlocked almost £500,000 of liquidity in less than two months—without borrowing a single pound. The bank meeting was cancelled. What looked like a funding crisis was, in fact, a working capital problem in disguise.

This paradox—where businesses cry for outside finance while sitting on hidden cash within their own operations—is far more common than most owners admit. Debt and equity are often viewed as the heroic lifelines of commerce, but the cheapest, fastest, and least dilutive source of cash is already inside the system: working capital. Every invoice, every payable, every day of stock sitting idle carries within it a choice: to free liquidity or to tie it up. The discipline of unlocking it is less glamorous than securing a new investor, but it is infinitely more powerful.

Working capital is the bloodstream of a company. Unlike external funding, it does not require covenants, board seats, or collateral—it requires attention, persistence, and negotiation. When receivables are collected swiftly, suppliers' terms are balanced wisely, and stock levels match reality rather than optimism, the firm effectively *raises* capital without debt or dilution. It is the alchemy of turning timing into cash.

The impact is startling when quantified. Imagine a business with £10 million in annual revenue, operating on 60-day receivables, 30-day payables, and 60 days of inventory. Its cash conversion cycle is 90 days, meaning that a full quarter of revenue is locked up in transit at any moment—£2.5 million frozen in the pipes. Tightening receivables by 15 days, negotiating an extra 10 days with suppliers, and cutting stock by a fortnight shrinks the cycle by over a month. That alone can release upwards of £800,000. To borrow the same sum from a bank might take months of negotiation, bind the firm in covenants, and cost tens of thousands in interest.

The lesson is sharp: every day shaved from the cycle is worth cash in the bank, and that cash is as real as any loan. A founder who improves terms has, in practical effect, just "raised" a round—without ceding equity or stacking up debt. But unlike raising money, which is often celebrated as a badge of honour, working capital discipline is invisible. Customers may not notice, suppliers may grumble, staff may complain about stricter credit checks—but the balance sheet transforms.

Examples abound across industries. In construction, contractors who demand 30 per cent upfront deposits drastically reduce the financing strain of long projects. In software services, firms that bill monthly in advance rather than arrears can fund growth without a credit line. In retail, chain operators who shave even a week off supplier payments across hundreds of stores release millions in aggregate. In each case, the business owner has a choice: to chase an investor pitch or to adjust the levers of the cycle.

Of course, there is a philosophical tension at play. Debt and equity feel like injections of new possibility, while working capital adjustments feel like restraint—chasing invoices, haggling for terms, cutting inventory optimism. The former promises expansion; the latter demands discipline. Yet discipline is expansion's foundation. No lender respects a business that cannot collect its receivables; no investor will admire a founder who raises capital only to squander it propping up poor payment habits. Fixing the cycle first is not optional housekeeping; it is the test of whether a firm deserves capital at all.

The psychological barrier is as real as the financial one. Entrepreneurs often delay tough conversations with customers who owe them money, fearing to sour relationships. They hesitate to push suppliers for better terms, worrying about leverage. They treat stock buffers as security blankets rather than cash drains. And so, instead of facing these frictions, they call the bank or court investors. But courage in these micro-negotiations compounds into freedom: the business that insists politely but firmly on being paid is the one that can survive the lean month without panicking.

The question, then, is not whether to raise external finance but when. The sequence matters. Fix the working capital cycle first—*prove* that the business can generate liquidity from its own operations—before even considering loans or equity. Only then does outside capital become a lever for growth, rather than a crutch for dysfunction.

Working capital is not glamorous. It does not make headlines. But it is the difference between a firm that lives at the mercy of banks and one that commands its own fate. The challenge for every entrepreneur is whether they will accept the discipline of fixing the cycle before raising—or whether they will remain forever in search of cash that was always within their reach.

And so the unresolved question lingers: before you draft the next pitch deck or loan application, have you truly counted the cash already sitting idle in your cycle? Or are you about to surrender control for money you didn't need to raise?

Debt, equity, revenue-based — Compare cost, control, and cadence of options. Flag red-line clauses to avoid. Match instruments to cash flows. Choose with eyes open.

When the founders of a promising software company in Bristol met with two investors on the same day, they were presented with two radically different offers. The first was a venture capital firm promising £5 million in equity at a valuation that would leave the founders minority owners within three years. The second was a bank offering £2 million in loans, secured against both company assets and personal guarantees. Days later, a third proposal arrived: a revenue-based financier prepared to advance £1.5 million, to be repaid as a small percentage of monthly sales. Each proposal glimmered with opportunity. Each concealed risks that could determine whether the founders would one day control a thriving business—or watch it slip away from them.

Such moments crystallise the essence of capital choices. Money is not neutral. The form it takes dictates not only the financial costs borne, but also the cadence of repayment, the degree of control retained, and the very culture of decision-making. To treat all capital as equal is a category error; the entrepreneur who conflates debt with equity, or revenue-based finance with either, is like a sailor navigating by stars without knowing which hemisphere he is in.

Debt is the oldest and, in many ways, the most straightforward. It is contractual, finite, and—if well-matched to cash flows—predictable. A term loan or revolving credit facility, with fixed interest and repayment schedules, can be a precise instrument: borrow £1 million, pay £50,000 in annual interest, and repay principal over five years. The clarity is attractive. Yet debt is also rigid. Should sales falter, the obligation does not flex. Red-line clauses—personal guarantees, aggressive covenants on coverage ratios, restrictions on further borrowing—can quickly turn a prudent instrument into a straitjacket. For many small firms, the risk is not the cost of debt but its inflexibility when volatility hits.

Equity, by contrast, demands no scheduled repayment. It is capital at its most forgiving of fluctuations—if revenues collapse one quarter, no cheques are due. But its price is invisible at the outset and astronomical in hindsight. Selling 20 per cent of a company today may feel painless when valuations are modest; a decade later, that same slice might represent hundreds of millions lost. Equity alters the balance of power. Investors may demand board seats, veto rights, liquidation preferences, or anti-dilution protections. These red-line clauses can quietly erode founder control, turning the entrepreneur into an operator executing someone else's strategy. The allure of equity is its patience; the danger is its permanence.

Revenue-based finance, a modern hybrid, attempts to balance flexibility with discipline. Here, the financier advances capital in exchange for a fixed percentage of monthly revenues—say, 5 per cent—until an agreed multiple of the original loan has been repaid. When sales soar, repayments accelerate; when sales dip, the burden lightens. For businesses with high gross margins and recurring revenues—subscription software, e-commerce brands—this alignment with sales cadence can be elegant. Yet the effective cost can be steep, often exceeding that of bank debt if growth is rapid, and terms may still conceal pitfalls: minimum repayment floors, warrants, or compounding fees that mimic equity's dilution without its upside.

The crucial insight is that capital must be matched to cash flows. A long-cycle construction firm, with uneven lump-sum receipts, may choke on rigid monthly debt service; equity or milestone-linked revenue financing may be more appropriate. A high-turnover retailer, by contrast, can thrive on a bank line matched to inventory cycles. A software-as-a-service company with recurring monthly subscriptions might find revenue-based finance the least intrusive. The wrong match is deadly: debt layered on volatile revenues invites default; equity raised to cover short-term working capital drains ownership for no strategic gain.

Control is not only a legal construct but also a cultural one. The founder who takes on debt retains autonomy but lives under constant pressure to meet obligations. The founder who raises equity gains breathing space but must negotiate every strategic pivot with external shareholders. The one who chooses revenue-based finance sits in between, trading a slice of future sales for present relief. Each path reshapes how decisions are made, who must be convinced, and how risks are tolerated.

Red-line clauses demand particular vigilance. In debt, beware covenants that trigger default for minor variances, cross-default provisions that drag down healthy subsidiaries, or demands for personal guarantees that risk private bankruptcy. In equity, scrutinise liquidation preferences that return investors multiples before founders see a pound, or anti-dilution clauses that punish successively lower rounds. In revenue-based finance, watch for hidden warrants, opaque fee structures, or repayment floors that transform flexibility into rigidity. The art of choosing capital lies as much in what one refuses as in what one accepts.

Philosophically, these choices raise deeper questions about time, ownership, and trust. Debt assumes the future will resemble the present closely enough to honour fixed promises. Equity assumes that long-term alignment with investors will survive shifting markets and ambitions. Revenue-based finance assumes a middle ground—that risk and reward can be shared dynamically in the rhythm of sales. Each embodies a different relationship with uncertainty. The wise entrepreneur does not ask only "how much money can I raise?" but also "what future am I committing myself to by raising it this way?"

The danger, as countless cautionary tales attest, is to see capital as a commodity rather than a covenant. Once accepted, it dictates outcomes as surely as strategy does. The founders in Bristol faced this truth. The bank's loan offered clarity but shackled them with guarantees. The venture capital term sheet offered abundance but stripped them of eventual control. The revenue-based deal seemed modest but offered breathing space without dilution. Which they chose is less important than how they chose: with eyes open, instruments matched to their cash flows, and a firm refusal to sign away control casually.

And so the lingering question remains: when the next offer of capital arrives at your table—debt, equity, or revenue-based—will you see it for what it truly is, or will you be blinded by the surface glow of numbers? The cost of a misstep is not just money. It is the shape of the future itself.

Banker's packet — Prepare the one-pager lenders read. Cover cycle, coverage, and covenants you can live with. Present like a calm operator. Increase the odds of a yes.

When a business owner sits across from a banker, the room is not equal. The banker has files of clients to review, dozens of proposals to consider, and only minutes to form a view. The entrepreneur has one chance. Often, the fate of an application rests not on a 40-page business plan, but on a single sheet of paper—the one-pager that distils the company's financial reality and its discipline. In lending, clarity is currency. Those who master it multiply their odds of hearing the one word they need: yes.

History offers countless lessons in presentation. In the 19th century, railway magnates secured vast sums for track and infrastructure not by overwhelming investors with engineering blueprints, but by issuing crisp prospectuses that captured the essence of their enterprise. The best ones conveyed cycles of income, debt coverage, and governance in spare prose and clean figures. Their success was not built on verbosity but on the confidence exuded by simplicity. The principle endures: the shorter the attention span of the gatekeeper, the greater the power of precision.

The banker's packet must achieve several things at once. First, it must map the operating cycle—how cash flows in and out, from receivables to payables, from stock purchases to sales receipts. Lenders are not impressed by visions of future dominance if the present cycle is opaque. They want to know: when does money arrive, how reliable is it, and how long does it linger before obligations fall due? A one-pager that demonstrates mastery of this rhythm signals operational competence more persuasively than any pitch deck filled with projections.

Next comes coverage. A banker will ask: how will this borrower repay us under stress? Here, ratios matter—debt service coverage, interest coverage, and free cash flow margins. But beyond the numbers lies narrative discipline: show that repayments are not balanced on a knife-edge of optimistic forecasts, but supported by historical performance and tested scenarios. A calm operator does not exaggerate strengths; they acknowledge vulnerabilities while demonstrating buffers. This candour builds trust more than glossy optimism ever could.

Covenants form the third pillar. Too often, desperate borrowers accept clauses they neither fully understand nor can realistically maintain: covenants that demand pristine balance sheets in turbulent industries, or that restrict future borrowing to the point of strangling growth. A strong one-pager does not hide from covenants but frames them. It sets out the terms the borrower can live with—ratios they know they can maintain, restrictions that align with their strategy—and politely resists overreach. This is not obstinacy; it is prudence. Bankers respect applicants who know their red lines, because such clarity reduces future conflict.

The structure of the document itself reveals much about the operator. A chaotic, over-designed sheet signals chaos in management. A calm, ordered layout—clear headings, concise bullet points, essential numbers—signals discipline. The reader must be able to scan the page in seconds and grasp the cycle, coverage, and covenants. Anything more is clutter. Anything less suggests unreadiness.

Examples abound of how this subtle discipline alters outcomes. A manufacturing firm seeking £3 million to upgrade equipment prepared a glossy 60-slide presentation brimming with growth forecasts. It failed. Months later, with the guidance of a finance director, they presented a one-pager that laid out their receivables days, payables days, inventory turns, and the exact debt service coverage they could guarantee under a conservative scenario. This time, the loan was approved within a fortnight. Nothing in the fundamentals had changed—only the way they were presented.

What underpins the banker's packet is not mere formatting but philosophy: an operator who is calm under scrutiny signals reliability under stress. Lenders know that businesses rarely travel in straight lines; turbulence is inevitable. The question is not whether volatility will come, but whether the borrower will remain composed when it does. A well-crafted one-pager demonstrates exactly that—by distilling complexity into clarity, it shows that the operator can sift signal from noise.

Yet here lies the paradox: in an age of instant data, when lenders have more information at their fingertips than ever before, the one-pager still matters. Why? Because abundance of data breeds impatience. Bankers will not wade through detail unless compelled by clarity. The one-pager is not a substitute for due diligence; it is the doorway to it. Without it, the process halts before it begins.

The entrepreneur preparing this document must ask themselves: if a stranger knew nothing about my business, could they understand its rhythm, resilience, and red lines in under three minutes? If not, the packet is unfinished. And if unfinished, the odds of a yes diminish.

So the enduring question is this: when your business stands before the banker, will you hand over a blizzard of detail—

or the single page that makes them lean forward and think, "This is someone who knows their numbers, knows their limits, and knows how to keep control"? The answer may be worth millions.

Use of proceeds — State exactly what the money buys and how it returns. Track weekly after funding. Prevent drift. Prove the thesis with cash.

When a business secures fresh capital—whether from a bank, investor, or alternative lender—the euphoria can be deceptive. What feels like victory is, in truth, an obligation. Every pound borrowed or invested arrives with an unspoken demand: prove that this money will multiply, not evaporate. The difference between those who ascend and those who falter lies not in the size of the cheque, but in the discipline of its deployment.

History is littered with examples of companies that raised funds only to squander them through drift. During the dot-com boom of the late 1990s, countless start-ups raised millions on the promise of digital transformation. Few could explain, in simple terms, how each dollar of spend would return in sales, margin, or market durability. Office chairs, advertising blitzes, speculative hires—their "use of proceeds" was vague. When markets tightened, the absence of a clear link between money spent and money earned left them exposed. By contrast, the firms that survived were those that tied every expenditure to a thesis: this investment buys *this* capability, which generates *this* return, within *this* time frame.

The phrase *use of proceeds* may sound bureaucratic, but it is the fulcrum of financial credibility. To state clearly what the money will buy—and how it will be repaid—forces a business to translate ambition into arithmetic. Will £100,000 fund additional stock that turns four times a year at a 25% gross margin, generating £100,000 in gross profit? Will £250,000 in software development create a feature that expands conversion rates by 10%, unlocking £500,000 in incremental revenue within 18 months? Vague assertions inspire little trust; quantified logic builds it.

Weekly tracking after funding is where theory meets reality. The temptation, once cash arrives, is to let monitoring slip—to assume that because funds are in the bank, discipline can be looser. The opposite is true. Money burns quietly and invisibly; drift happens in increments too small to notice until the hole is deep. A weekly review of how funds are spent, compared against the original thesis, ensures that deviations are caught early. Was that marketing campaign delivering the promised lead flow? Are customer deposits arriving in line with expectations? Are savings from a new supplier being realised in cash, not just in projections?

Consider the example of a construction company that secured £500,000 in growth funding. Instead of declaring "we will use the money for expansion," management broke it into precise allocations: £200,000 for equipment, £150,000 for working capital to support larger contracts, £100,000 for a dedicated project manager, and £50,000 for contingency. Each line item was tied to a measurable outcome: number of contracts supported, reduction in project overruns, additional revenue captured. By updating a simple weekly dashboard, they could show lenders and themselves whether the thesis held. This transparency not only reduced internal drift but strengthened external trust; lenders extended additional credit later on, impressed by the clarity.

The philosophical underpinning is straightforward yet profound: capital is not fuel to be burned; it is a hypothesis to be tested. Each allocation is a claim about how the future will unfold. To prove the thesis with cash is to respect both the investor and the enterprise by recognising money as evidence, not assumption. A company that can point to each pound spent and say, "Here is what it bought, here is how it returned," builds resilience far beyond the balance sheet. It builds credibility in markets where trust is rare.

Yet the tension persists: how granular should the use of proceeds be? Too vague, and discipline evaporates. Too rigid, and flexibility disappears. The art lies in balancing clarity with adaptability. State the destination and milestones with precision, but allow tactical adjustments in the route. For instance, a business might allocate £100,000 to reduce customer acquisition costs. If a new channel unexpectedly outperforms, funds can shift—but the purpose, lowering CAC, remains constant.

In this sense, *use of proceeds* is not merely financial reporting; it is a philosophy of leadership. It reflects how an organisation treats money as a strategic instrument rather than an emotional comfort. It demands candour with staff and stakeholders, because clarity about where funds are going and how they are performing prevents suspicion and drift. And it obliges founders to confront the uncomfortable question: if this spend does not return as expected, will we stop, reallocate, or double down?

The paradox is clear. Capital, when used with discipline, magnifies capability. When handled carelessly, it amplifies fragility. The act of stating exactly what the money buys and how it returns is not just administrative housekeeping—it is a crucible of strategy.

So the lingering question is this: when the next pound arrives, will it be treated as a resource to be consumed, or as a thesis to be tested and proved with cash? The answer reveals not only the fate of the money, but the fate of the enterprise itself.

Chapter 10
The One-Page Board Pack

In 1961, John F. Kennedy stood before Congress and set a national goal: to land a man on the Moon before the decade's end. What is often forgotten is not the grandeur of the vision, but the way it was managed. NASA learned quickly that sprawling documents and endless committees would cripple progress. Instead, the agency condensed its decision-making into short, sharp updates: a few critical objectives, one or two telling metrics, and clear accountability. The audacity of the mission demanded not more words, but more clarity.

Most boards today wrestle with the opposite problem. A deck arrives in their inbox two days before the meeting, swollen with charts and bullet points. Eighty slides later, the essential question—what must we decide now?—remains obscured. Directors, drained of attention, default to tactical quibbles. Meetings drift, time dissolves, and the hardest decisions are postponed. For founders and executives, this is not just a nuisance; it is a slow erosion of momentum.

The paradox is stark: the more data we generate, the less focused our conversations become. Boards do not fail because they lack information; they fail because they drown in it. What is needed is not another presentation template, but a philosophy of compression: reduce the noise until only the signal remains. A *one-page board pack*—a single sheet that crystallises the six decisions that truly matter, each paired with one decisive metric—becomes not a gimmick, but a discipline.

The discipline rests on three elements. First, structure: a traffic-light dashboard that makes thresholds visible and immediate. Green signals stability. Amber prompts investigation. Red demands action. Status is not hidden in narrative but displayed in colour, driving urgency without theatrics. Second, narrative: a short written explanation beneath each decision point. No meandering digressions, no "let's come back to that." Each section closes with a dated next step. Talk turns into commitments, and commitments into a record that is revisited. Third, cadence: the weekly loop. By tying board packs into a Friday ritual, decisions compound over time. Small corrections, made consistently, outpace grand strategy sessions made rarely.

Why does this matter now, more than ever? Because uncertainty punishes delay. Companies operate in markets where conditions shift monthly, sometimes weekly. A board that meets armed with sprawling decks risks paralysis just when clarity is most needed. The one-page pack, by contrast, institutionalises sharpness. It signals to investors, staff, and lenders that leadership is not hiding behind slides but confronting reality with precision.

And yet, the simplicity of the form conceals its difficulty. To compress complexity into a page is to choose—ruthlessly—what matters. Which six decisions rise above the noise? Which metric cuts through the vanity measures to reveal the true state of affairs? Which commitments will stand the test of time when the meeting is over? These are not formatting questions; they are questions of leadership, of courage, of what it means to turn governance from performance into action.

The promise of the one-page board pack is not that it makes meetings shorter, but that it makes decisions sharper. It strips away the comfort of endless analysis and replaces it with consequence. The unanswered challenge is whether boards and executives are willing to embrace the discomfort of focus: to abandon vanity, to welcome visibility, and to let numbers—not narratives—carry the weight of proof.

The next chapter will test this. For the one-page pack is not a document to be admired, but a mirror held up to leadership. What, after all, belongs on your single page? And what, by omission, are you willing to admit no longer matters?

From vanity to clarity — Cut decks to six decisions that matter. Pair each with one telling metric. Stop meetings wandering through charts. Keep everyone on the same page.

The most expensive part of a board meeting is not the catered lunch, the travel, or the glossy deck of slides. It is the wasted hour that never produces a decision. Many executives have sat through these rituals: sixty-page slide decks filled with charts that tell a story no one can follow, a meandering conversation that never settles on the essential, and a sense of fatigue that arrives long before clarity does. The paradox is that the more information we assemble, the less we actually decide. Abundance becomes its own form of blindness.

Consider the case of a mid-sized retailer that, in the midst of declining margins, delivered a 92-slide presentation to its board. The data was immaculate—segmented by region, broken down by customer demographics, sliced into hundreds of charts. Yet the board left without agreeing on whether to reduce store count, renegotiate supplier contracts, or double down on e-commerce. In drowning the board in evidence, management had obscured the very crossroads the company stood upon. Weeks were lost, competitors moved, and cash continued to leak. What was missing was not information, but focus.

Focus is what transforms a board pack from vanity into clarity. The rule is disarmingly simple: cut the deck to six decisions that matter, and pair each with one telling metric. Six—not because the number is magical, but because it forces prioritisation. If you cannot condense your business into six active decisions, you do not yet understand it. One metric—not a cluster—because each decision should hinge on a single piece of evidence that makes further debate unnecessary.

This discipline is harder than it sounds. Most leaders conflate *activity* with *decisions*. They report on what has been done—marketing campaigns launched, new hires made, product features shipped—rather than framing what must be decided. This is vanity: evidence of effort, not of consequence. Clarity begins when the frame shifts. Instead of "we launched three campaigns last quarter," the decision is "do we double marketing spend in Q2?" The telling metric might be customer acquisition cost compared with lifetime value. Everything else is supporting noise.

By narrowing focus, boards move from wandering conversations to consequential debate. Instead of a scatter of questions—why did churn tick up in one segment, what explains last week's revenue dip, how is product adoption tracking—directors are confronted with the decision that matters: do we invest further in retention initiatives, or accept current churn levels and allocate capital elsewhere? The telling metric—say, net revenue retention—anchors the discussion. The board leaves not with more questions, but with a collective decision.

The philosophical underpinning is as old as governance itself: clarity requires sacrifice. Just as a great editor knows which paragraphs to cut, a great leader knows which numbers to exclude. Vanity metrics—those that look impressive but change little—must be stripped away. Monthly website visits, social media impressions, vague satisfaction scores: these can be displayed in appendices, but they do not belong on the page where decisions are made. What belongs is the sharp metric that binds decision to consequence.

Consider the example of an early-stage SaaS company debating whether to hire an additional sales team. The vanity approach is to present a cascade of graphs: pipeline size, number of demos, customer count, marketing spend, website conversions. The clarity approach is to distil all of this into one question: should we add sales capacity now? The one telling metric is the payback period on customer acquisition. If current acquisition costs are recouped in less than twelve months, then the decision has a clear case. If not, the answer is equally clear. The difference is that clarity drives action, while vanity sustains conversation.

Of course, this discipline demands courage. To present only six decisions with one metric each is to accept that you will be judged on the strength of those decisions. There is nowhere to hide, no blizzard of slides to diffuse accountability. Yet that is precisely why it works. Boards and leadership teams do not exist to admire charts; they exist to decide how to allocate scarce resources—capital, time, people—under uncertainty. A lean pack forces everyone to confront that truth.

This does not mean ignoring nuance. Every decision lives within context. But context should serve the decision, not the other way around. A two-page appendix can carry supporting analysis for those who need it, but the board's energy should remain pinned to the six questions that matter most this week, this quarter, this moment in the company's life. In this way, the meeting becomes not a recital but a council of judgement.

What emerges, over time, is a cultural shift. Meetings are no longer battlegrounds of interpretation, but crucibles of choice. Directors stop nit-picking charts because there are no charts to nit-pick—only decisions to weigh. Executives stop performing their efforts for applause and begin presenting their dilemmas for resolution. The board becomes not a theatre but a compass, helping the company to move in deliberate steps rather than circling in data.

Yet an unresolved question always lingers: which six decisions will you choose? It is not a question of formatting, but of leadership. To know what belongs on the page, you must know what truly moves your business, what risks you can accept, and where your scarce resources must go next. Clarity is not a template; it is a test of discernment.

The practice of cutting from vanity to clarity does not merely sharpen meetings; it sharpens the company itself. The unanswered tension is whether leaders are willing to bear the discipline—whether they will continue to cloak indecision in pages of charts, or whether they will distil their business into the six questions that matter, and finally decide.

Traffic-light dashboard — Build thresholds and assign owners. Green you maintain, amber you investigate, red you act. Make status visual and immediate. Drive the next move.

In aviation, a cockpit is built to prevent hesitation. Lights flash red when action cannot be deferred; amber signals require swift investigation; green allows the pilot to fly on.

No pilot would tolerate a dashboard that reported hundreds of numbers without hierarchy. Yet in business, many leaders ask their teams to navigate precisely such a cockpit—spreadsheets and charts sprawling across pages, with no clear sense of what is urgent, what is stable, and what is sliding. The paradox is sharp: in organisations that prize speed, the flow of information is often designed for paralysis.

The traffic-light dashboard is an antidote. It takes the sprawling complexity of a company's operations and compresses it into a universal language: green, amber, red. A dashboard does not try to mirror reality in all its detail; it reduces reality to thresholds. That reduction is not distortion but clarity, because decisions rarely hinge on decimals. They hinge on whether something is healthy, questionable, or broken. And when you make that status visual and immediate, you strip away the room for dithering.

But thresholds mean nothing unless they are defined with precision. Too many dashboards hide behind vague colours—turnover is "amber" because it feels concerning, cash is "green" because no one has complained. The discipline lies in numeric triggers: cash below thirty days of coverage is red, debtor days above fifty is amber, conversion rates above ten per cent stay green. These thresholds translate anxiety into objective signal. They also force foresight: an amber light does not mean "panic," it means "investigate before this turns red." In doing so, the organisation learns to see fragility before it becomes collapse.

Assigning owners is the second discipline. A dashboard without owners is theatre: lights change, but no one moves. When each threshold is tied to a name, accountability sharpens. If cash turns amber, the finance lead is on the hook to investigate. If customer churn ticks red, the head of retention acts. Ownership is not about blame—it is about clarity of response. Without it, status reports degrade into commentary; with it, they become commitments.

The philosophical tension is between simplification and reality. Businesses are complex; no set of colours can capture nuance. But the point of a traffic-light dashboard is not to tell the whole story. It is to surface the few signals that demand energy now. Think of a hospital: thousands of data points exist for a patient, but the monitor at the bedside shows heart rate, oxygen, blood pressure. The aim is not exhaustiveness but survival. The same holds for a company—simplify to the signals without which all else collapses.

Practical examples abound. A construction firm built a dashboard that tracked three lights: cash days, project overruns, and safety incidents. When safety turned amber, managers investigated within hours, preventing red events. Over a year, incidents halved, while cash stability improved simply because leaders no longer tolerated creeping debtor delays. Or consider a digital agency that tied amber lights on client retention to immediate customer interviews.

Rather than waiting for cancellation, they acted on warning signs, saving contracts that might have quietly expired. The discipline of colour coding forced them into cadence.

There is also a cultural dimension. When status is made visual, politics recedes. It is difficult to spin a red indicator into good news; the light compels candour. Equally, it creates relief when metrics are green. Teams no longer burn energy defending stable processes; they simply maintain them. Attention concentrates on the amber and red. Meetings shift from posturing to action because the colour dictates urgency. The dashboard becomes a silent but powerful chairperson, steering the conversation towards the next move.

Yet one must guard against complacency. A green dashboard is not a license for relaxation—it is an instruction to maintain discipline. Too often, organisations grow lax when all lights are green, only to be shocked when they swing to red. Maintenance is invisible work, but it is what keeps the system from collapse. The wisdom of the dashboard is not just in triggering action, but in reminding teams that green itself is a state that requires vigilance.

The deeper question remains: can a company accept the humility of thresholds? Many leaders resist reducing their world to colours, fearing it oversimplifies. But the power of the dashboard is precisely in its reduction. It is not designed for vanity; it is designed for movement. It is the discipline of deciding, in advance, what numbers matter most, what levels signal danger, and who must respond. In a world of infinite data, the courage to reduce is itself a competitive advantage.

The unresolved challenge, then, is not whether dashboards work—they do—but whether leaders will live by them. Will they obey the red light, act when amber flickers, and avoid the temptation to drown green in complacency? A traffic-light dashboard is only as strong as the discipline behind it. The question each company must face is whether they will treat their dashboard as decoration, or as the cockpit by which they steer their survival.

Narrative and next actions — Replace meandering talk with a short written narrative. End each section with a dated commitment. Turn discussion into decisions. Record and revisit.

In 1961, President John F. Kennedy declared that America would land a man on the moon before the decade was out. The statement was not a meandering conversation point. It was a narrative with a deadline. Its power did not lie in poetry or optimism but in its precision: a singular mission, a defined endpoint, and an implicit commitment that progress would be measured. The Apollo programme was vast and complex, yet its clarity was born not from endless debate but from the discipline of narrative direction combined with dated action.

Contrast that with the experience of most boardrooms and management meetings today. Leaders enter with intentions to decide, yet discussions fragment into anecdotes, tangents, and abstractions. Charts are examined, opinions exchanged, but as the hours pass, the air thickens with unresolved threads. Everyone departs with the illusion of progress but nothing that binds the future. The absence is not intelligence, but discipline—the discipline to condense complexity into a short narrative, to end each section with a clear commitment, and to record that decision so it can be revisited. Without it, meetings are little more than performance.

The paradox is striking: organisations brim with data, yet struggle to tell the story of what it means. They are rich in dialogue but poor in decision. The narrative-and-actions discipline resolves both tensions. A short written narrative forces clarity of thought: it demands that the author distil the issue into essence rather than scatter it across slides. When paired with a dated commitment—what will be done, by whom, and by when—it transforms meetings from forums of speculation into engines of accountability.

Consider the case of Amazon. Famously, its senior meetings begin not with slide decks but with six-page narratives. Attendees sit in silence, reading the document, before discussion begins. The narrative anchors the conversation: it ensures that everyone has absorbed the same framing and that debate is about the content, not about interpreting the chart. The shift from visuals to prose is not aesthetic—it is cognitive. Writing reveals where thinking is thin. Numbers without a story can be bent to any interpretation; a narrative resists such evasion.

Yet narrative alone is insufficient. Without next actions, it becomes another story in a sea of stories. This is why the discipline demands that each section closes with a dated commitment. Decisions without dates decay. By attaching time to every action, ambiguity collapses into obligation. The question changes from *what should we do?* to *what will be done by next week?* The human mind responds differently to commitments when they are tethered to dates: they move from the abstract to the urgent.

Philosophically, this approach reflects a deeper truth about human institutions. Talk, left unchecked, drifts toward self-justification. We rehearse ideas to display intelligence, to negotiate standing, to delay the discomfort of choice. The narrative-and-actions framework strips away that indulgence. It is a mirror held up to the group: what is the issue, what is the story, what is the commitment? In this way, it institutionalises candour. Where the narrative is vague, it forces rethinking. Where the commitment is missing, it forces the group to confront its own hesitation.

Real-world practice demonstrates its potency. A European technology firm adopted a one-page narrative template for its executive meetings: each agenda item had to be explained in under 300 words, followed by a line stating the proposed decision and the dated commitment if agreed. Within six months, the average length of meetings halved, but the number of actual decisions tripled. Managers reported higher trust because every week, previous commitments were revisited—those met reinforced credibility, those missed prompted investigation. The system converted words into an observable trail of actions.

There is a counterargument: some claim that narrative writing slows down fast-moving organisations. Why not rely on instinct, improvisation, or informal agreements? But history shows that the greatest accelerators are clarity and accountability. A military unit in the field may thrive on oral orders, but even there, the principle is the same: a commander issues a concise narrative of intent and binds it to time. In civilian organisations, where complexity multiplies and accountability disperses, the risk of drift is greater. Writing does not slow—it accelerates by preventing rework, confusion, and endless revisiting of the same undecided issues.

Equally important is the act of recording and revisiting. Organisations have short memories. Promises made in one quarter are often forgotten by the next. A narrative archive provides institutional memory—it allows the team to see not only what was decided, but why. Over time, this builds more than efficiency; it builds culture. People internalise the expectation that words must turn into commitments, and commitments will be tracked. The culture shifts from performative talk to consequential talk.

At its heart, this discipline respects time—the scarcest resource of modern professionals. Every meandering discussion squanders collective hours that can never be reclaimed. A short narrative honours those hours by making sure they are spent in pursuit of clarity. A dated commitment honours them again by ensuring the time produces a return. Record and revisit honours them a third time by ensuring the lessons compound.

The unresolved tension, however, lies in courage. Writing a narrative exposes the author's thinking to scrutiny; attaching a date exposes their accountability. Many prefer the comfort of ambiguity, the shield of endless discussion. The true challenge is not the mechanics of the method, but the willingness to live by its implications. Will leaders accept the discipline of writing instead of talking? Will teams embrace the discomfort of dates?

That is the question every serious organisation must face: do we want to be a place where words float, or a place where words bind? The answer will not be found in another meeting. It will be found in the discipline of narrative and next actions, and in whether those who claim to lead are willing to commit their words to the page, and their promises to time.

The weekly loop — Tie the pack back to Friday cadence. Ensure information becomes movement. Protect the ritual from drift. Compound small, correct moves.

On 10 May 1940, Winston Churchill became Prime Minister of Britain at a moment when the nation teetered on the edge of catastrophe. In his first days, he established the War

Cabinet's discipline: daily briefings, weekly loops of action and review, and relentless cadence. Every Friday, ministers knew that the prior week's promises would be revisited, and next steps defined. It was not the brilliance of any one decision that sustained Britain through its darkest hours, but the constancy of a loop that converted information into movement, week after week, until momentum was unbreakable.

Modern businesses often underestimate the same principle. They overvalue the drama of large strategic shifts while undervaluing the quiet power of steady cadence. They create beautiful board packs, distribute dense decks, and spend hours in discussion, but unless those rituals are bound to a loop—a rhythm where talk becomes trackable action—the energy dissipates. It is not information that moves organisations forward, but the conversion of information into small, correct moves repeated consistently. The weekly loop is that conversion engine.

The paradox is that most organisations already have recurring meetings, yet very few have true loops. A meeting without a loop is like a river without banks: the water flows, but the direction is aimless. The weekly loop provides containment. It ties information back to commitments, ensures progress is reviewed within a predictable timeframe, and protects the discipline of execution from the entropy of drift.

The choice of cadence matters. Weekly is both short enough to sustain urgency and long enough to allow meaningful progress. Daily meetings often breed fatigue and superficial updates, while monthly ones allow drift to accumulate. Friday, in particular, has symbolic and practical power. It closes the week with clarity, frames the weekend with reflection, and launches Monday with momentum. Teams enter the next cycle not with vague intentions, but with visible commitments recorded, revisited, and refined.

Consider the practice of Toyota's famed production system. Much attention is given to its tools—kanban cards, just-in-time delivery, lean manufacturing—but its real genius lay in cadence. Each week, factory teams reviewed metrics, examined deviations, and committed to small adjustments. These loops compounded over time, producing an organisation that did not rely on dramatic interventions, but on relentless improvement. The lesson applies equally outside manufacturing: cadence institutionalises learning, turning the abstract idea of continuous improvement into a lived habit.

The weekly loop also creates accountability without requiring constant confrontation. When a team knows that every Friday, prior commitments will be revisited, accountability becomes a property of the system, not a matter of personality. Leaders no longer need to chase or scold; the loop itself exposes progress or its absence. This shift is profound. It replaces episodic heroics with systemic discipline, fostering a culture where credibility is earned not by speeches but by the steady honouring of commitments.

Yet the loop is fragile. It drifts when meetings become social rather than operational, when updates are tolerated without actions, or when the cadence itself is allowed to slip. Every leader has felt the temptation to cancel the Friday ritual "just this once." But the missed week is rarely recovered. Rituals protect institutions precisely because they endure when convenience argues otherwise. In protecting the weekly loop, leaders are not protecting a calendar entry but the compounding of discipline over time.

Philosophically, the loop embodies a tension between freedom and structure. Too much structure and the organisation feels rigid, suffocated by process. Too much freedom and drift takes hold, producing chaos masked as creativity. The weekly loop is a middle path: it provides a rhythm strong enough to channel energy but flexible enough to adapt. It is not bureaucracy—it is choreography. When done well, participants feel not constrained but synchronised.

The key to sustaining it is simplicity. The pack that ties into the loop must focus on essentials: decisions, metrics, actions. Overcomplication suffocates cadence. A six-page narrative, a dashboard with thresholds, and a short list of commitments suffice. More data does not equal more progress; in fact, it often overwhelms and paralyses. By keeping the loop lightweight, it remains live, resilient against the creep of vanity metrics and ornamental slides.

Over time, the compounding power of the weekly loop becomes visible. Each small, correct move builds on the last.

A pricing decision refined here, a hiring commitment honoured there, a cash threshold respected, a dispute resolved—each is minor in isolation, but transformative in sequence. The organisation becomes more trustworthy, more aligned, more predictable. Momentum ceases to be episodic and becomes institutional.

And yet, the unresolved question lingers: will leaders and teams embrace the humility of cadence over the seduction of drama? It is always easier to announce a bold strategy than to sustain the grind of weekly loops. But history and practice show the truth: empires endure, companies thrive, and teams succeed not because of a single grand move, but because they mastered the art of compounding small, correct moves, week after week.

The weekly loop is not glamorous. But it may be the most powerful force a business can harness. The test, as always, is discipline. Will the ritual hold? Or will drift win, as it so often does? That answer will determine not just the rhythm of a week, but the trajectory of an entire enterprise.

About the Author

Kenji Takahashi writes for founders who would rather build than posture. Raised between Osaka's shop-house pragmatism and the clean lines of contemporary design, he approaches finance the way an engineer approaches form: remove what does not serve function, and make the remaining parts work harder. His essays and workshops focus on the quiet levers—pricing, contribution margin, payment terms—that decide whether a small enterprise sleeps well or lives on the brink. He has spent years sitting at simple tables with owners, sketching 13-week cash views on paper napkins and turning them into weekly habits. Influenced by Edo-period ideas of frugality and craft as well as post-war management thought, his work favours clarity over glamour and cadence over drama. He believes a business earns the right to plan the future only after it learns to pay itself on time.

www.ingramcontent.com/pod-product-compliance
Lightning Source LLC
Chambersburg PA
CBHW031345230926
51848CB00002B/399
9789374120620